it’s in the post

3
NEW ZEALAND POSTA

it's in the post

the stories behind new zealand stamps

Richard wolfe

craig potton publishing

For Stan (1915–22)

acknowledgements

The author would like to thank Jane Connor for the opportunity to write this book and Sarah Elworthy for all her design skills.

The publishers would like to thank David Holmes at Auckland City Stamps (www.aucklandcitystamps.co.nz) for his help and generosity in loaning stamps; Patrick Brownsey and Becky Masters at Museum of New Zealand Te Papa Tongarewa for their help with materials from the New Zealand Post archive; Peter Deutschle at Spectra Graphics for his enthusiasm for the project and his technical expertise; and Sarah Elworthy for her wonderful design and careful attention to detail.

First published in 2010 by Craig Potton Publishing

Craig Potton Publishing
98 Vickerman Street, PO Box 555, Nelson, New Zealand
www.craigpotton.co.nz

Text and cover design: Sarah Elworthy
Prepress by Spectra Graphics, Auckland
Printed in China by Midas Printing International Ltd

ISBN 978 1 877517 28 0

contents

introduction

For New Zealanders born in the period following the Second World War, the collecting of postage stamps was a popular pastime. Also appealing to their acquisitive instincts were the free picture cards provided by the wily manufacturers of breakfast cereals. All these small images brought the exotic into the home, and stamps in particular came from places young New Zealanders could then only dream about. Affordable overseas travel awaited the arrival of the jet age, while the previous generation's only direct experience of the outside world may have been as a result of war service.

The keen stamp collector then saw the world neatly divided into two categories: British and foreign. The first, which naturally included us, was distinguished by depictions of the reigning monarch. In this regard New Zealanders were well catered for, and in 1953 the country produced special stamps to honour both the coronation and the historic visit here by the young Queen Elizabeth II. Then, two years later Her Majesty was part

A sense of speed is captured in this line drawing for the 1939 Express Delivery stamp, designed by James Berry. It depicts a Chrysler coupe, which was used for the delivery of correspondence in New Zealand's larger centres.

The 1939 Express Delivery stamp replaced a stamp which had been in use since 1903, following the establishment (on 1 January 1901) of the Post and Telegraph Office's express delivery and special messenger service.

of an issue marking the centenary of New Zealand's first adhesive postage stamp, the Full Face Queen of 1855. That stamp carried a profile portrait of Victoria, great-grandmother of the present monarch.

Images of Queen Victoria dominated New Zealand's stamps for the first 43 years. But in 1898 postal authorities took the bold step of recognising that stamps could serve another patriotic purpose, the promotion of the country's natural attractions, and so our first Pictorial set appeared. In addition to the obligatory images of kings and queens (with the exception of Edward VIII), stamps now began to acknowledge other aspects of New Zealand's history and development. Obvious subjects were the consequences of two world wars, as expressed by the Victory and Peace issues of 1920 and 1946, and centennials, including the country's recognition—in 1940—of 100 years since colonisation by Britain. In addition, new sets of Pictorials released in 1935 and 1960 were opportunities to introduce such themes as Maori subjects and native flowers.

But even with this broadening of scope, New Zealand's output of postage stamps was relatively modest, especially when compared to that maintained by certain 'foreign' countries. In fact, with the exception of the annual Health issues (introduced from 1929), New Zealand did not produce any new stamps in the period from 1926 to 1931. And more recently, there were some years in the early 1950s when the country was apparently unable to find any other subjects worthy of being celebrated on postage stamps.

Stamps can be regarded as indicators of how a country wishes to present itself to the outside world, and the responsibility for New Zealand's images has fallen to a select number of designers. For a significant part of the 20th century this field was dominated by just two individuals, James Berry and Leonard C. Mitchell. That it is a specialist skill was made abundantly clear in the early 1900s when several images by artists better known for their large oil paintings did not happily translate to the miniature scale demanded by postage stamps. Another significant development was the gradual transformation from decorative borders and ornamental devices to simpler compositions and plainer backgrounds. Designs now needed to be more immediately appealing, to command attention in a visually cluttered world.

As well as showcasing the nation's monarch and other distinctive features, stamps can also be more self-serving. An early example was the Penny Universal of 1901, which succeeded in its aim of encouraging New Zealanders to post more letters. Since then, stamps themselves have been

The lower values in the Decimal Pictorial set depicted native flora. They included the 2c Kaka beak, the 5c Clematis and the 7c Rata (designed by Allan Mitchell, Wellington), and the 2½c Kowhai (designed by Geoff Fuller, Havelock North).

the subject of further issues, as when celebrating anniversaries of the Full Face Queens. But a century after the Penny Universal, the amount of mail this country is now sending is decreasing. This decline was a world-wide phenomenon which had been apparent for a few years and, for economic reasons, might require a reduction in the frequency of New Zealand's mail deliveries.

Another change being experienced by postage stamps may be their popularity as collectibles. In August 2010 *The Guardian* newspaper reported a diversity of opinion as to whether stamps represented a sound investment, noting that the world's most sought-after stamp—a Swedish misprint from 1855—had not risen in value in the previous 15 years. Nevertheless, with a weight of 250 mg and a sale price of some £1.6 million, this small piece of (imperfectly) printed paper was worth a staggering £6.4 billion per kilogram, qualifying it as the most expensive object in the world by weight.

This overview of this country's stamps intentionally concentrates on their first century or so of development and takes advantage of the rich archives of New Zealand Post held by Te Papa Tongarewa Museum of New Zealand. Each stamp has a story to tell, both in the choice of the subject and the manner in which it has been interpreted. Their own history suggests there is a lot more to these small images than just a convenient means of prepaying postage.

In the days when New Zealand produced fewer stamps, the appearance of a new issue was likely to stimulate some heated public debate, especially if it involved a representation of the monarch. There may be less discussion on such matters nowadays, but there is no less pressure on stamps to maintain their visual appeal in this image-saturated age. New Zealand's stamps have long since broken out of the confines of decorative borders and traditional expectations, and now deal with subjects that earlier postal authorities could not have imagined. Stamps are under constant pressure to adjust and adapt, and collectively represent a vital record of social change. One hundred and fifty-five years on, they continue to be a highly effective means by which New Zealanders can both celebrate their own landscape and way of life, and send snapshots to the outside world.

Richard wolfe august 2010

New Zealand butterflies and moths were featured on the lower values of the 1970-71 Definitives. Shown here (above) are the 2c tussock butterfly, and (opposite) ½d glade copper butterfly and 1c red admiral butterfly, all designed by Enid Hunter.

1 full faces and sidefaces

Victoria

In January 1840 Captain William Hobson sailed across from New South Wales to the Bay of Islands in northern New Zealand. On the afternoon of the 30th he came ashore from HMS *Herald* at Kororareka (later renamed Russell) and at a public meeting read out a commission appointing him lieutenant-governor of New Zealand. He then arranged to meet with chiefs of the northern Maori tribes, and the Treaty of Waitangi was signed on 6 February. Copies of this document were circulated around the country for further signatures, and on 21 May 1840 Hobson proclaimed British sovereignty over all of New Zealand. Its citizens were now subjects of Her Majesty Victoria, Queen of the United Kingdom of Great Britain and Ireland. Significantly, New Zealand became a colony just two weeks after the issue in Britain of the Penny Black, the world's first prepaid adhesive postage stamp.

From 1862 the Full Face Queens were easier to separate when they appeared with perforations. The orange 2d was one of 11 different denominations and colours, ranging from 1d to 1/-.

Hobson arrived in the Bay of Islands with a number of officials,

NEW ZEALAND
POSTAGE
TWO PENCE

The first 6d Full Face stamp appeared (without perforations) in 1859, supplementing the original 1d, 2d and 1/-, which had been issued in 1855.

including the colony's first postmaster. At that time postage on mail was paid in cash, either by the sender or by the addressee. It was a slow and unsatisfactory system, but in late December 1850 the Governor, George Grey, announced new regulations recommending the introduction of a system of pre-payment by means of stamps. The new postal rates would be 2d for every letter not exceeding half an ounce in weight and 2d for every additional half ounce or fraction thereof. The planned regulations also allowed for printed newspapers to be sent free of postage, provided they were uncovered and included no writing or enclosures. There was also to be a special rate for soldiers and seamen, who were entitled to send letters provided they were signed by a commanding officer. But New Zealanders had to wait until they had postage stamps to avail themselves of these new regulations. Because of the lack of skills and equipment in this country, the stamps were designed and printed in London, by Messrs Perkins & Bacon, and arrived in Wellington in February 1855.

The pioneering Penny Black had carried an image of Queen Victoria, the inevitable choice when New Zealand introduced stamps of its own 15 years later. The image was based on a portrait by Swiss-born English artist Alfred Edward Chalon and showed the young queen in her royal robes of state, as worn for her first official duty, at the House of Lords on 17 July 1837. A watercolour copy of Chalon's portrait was made by English artist

Edward Henry Corbould and from this the stamp image was engraved on steel by William Humphrys. The original portrait, painted at Victoria's command and presented by her to her mother, is now believed to be in the Belgian Royal Collection. It became known as the 'Chalon head', and was the subject of numerous copies. It was a popular choice for postage stamps issued by British colonies, including Queensland, Tasmania, Canada, Nova Scotia, Natal and the Bahamas, as well as New Zealand.

Victoria's royal robes were described in detail by *The Times*: 'Over a white satin petticoat, embroidered with gold, the Queen wore a kirtie of crimson velvet trimmed with ermine in stripes, and gold lace. The robe was confined at the waist and shoulders with gold cords and tassels. Her Majesty had a diamond stomacher; on both arms strings of diamonds, and on the left an armlet, with the motto of the order of the garter. Her Majesty also wore the Riband, Badge, and Star of the Order, the two latter set in diamonds.' On her head the queen wore 'a splendid circlet of diamonds.' The upper sections of the robes and garter ribbon would be shown on the first New Zealand stamp, and the queen was given a mechanically produced background, as used on banknotes to thwart forgers. This image would come to be known as the Full Face Queen, although Her Majesty was turned and gazing somewhat to the left.

The first printing of the stamps was sent from London in September

The blue 2d Full Face, one of the set of New Zealand's first stamps, issued in 1855. In a portrait known as the 'Chalon head', Queen Victoria was depicted in her Royal Robes of State.

1854, and included 12,000 of the 1d, 66,000 of the 2d and 8,000 of the 1/-, along with plates for subsequent reprintings in New Zealand. They went on sale on 18 July 1855, and a week later the *Southern Cross* newspaper could report that the advantages of this system over money payments are 'universally acknowledged,' and that 'much inconvenience and loss of time will thereby be avoided.' But although New Zealand now had postage stamps, it was not compulsory to use them until 1 April 1862.

The original set of three was supplemented by a 6d stamp in 1859. Changes in overseas rates required the introduction of a 3d value in 1863 and a 4d two years later. The Chalon head was common to all, but there were many variations in colour, paper types, watermarks and perforations as a result of numerous local reprintings.

In 1873 the Full Face Queens were supplemented by a ½d stamp, for newspaper use. The design, based on a current British stamp, was engraved on wood in Melbourne and from this a plate was made in Wellington. It depicted a left-facing profile of Queen Victoria, and this was continued by a set of six designed in London and issued on 1 January 1874 to replace the Full Faces. On the new stamps, logically known as Sidefaces, the queen's head was placed within a variety of borders. A second set appeared in 1882, and these acknowledged a change in regulations, replacing the original 'postage' with 'postage and revenue' to indicate these stamps could also be used for the payment of government charges.

The Second Sidefaces included a 2½d stamp, which was issued in late December 1891 and came in for some colourful criticism. One commentator suggested that both the designer—A. E. Cousins—and the government had laid themselves open to a charge of 'high treason for their abominable caricature of our lady sovereign.' Her Majesty appeared to be suffering from 'the combined effects of a severe fight [sic] and an attack of mumps, the former having caused her hair to stand on end to the imminent danger of her miniature crown … while the latter has swelled her poor jaw to a porcine fatness.' As for other elements in the design, these were considered indistinct and appeared to include 'a canoe with an emu in the bow and a Maori with a parasol in the stern.' The same commentator summed up: 'The printing, colouring and get up of the stamp are atrocious.' Out of respect for friends at 'home', he would use two 1d stamps and a ½d one instead of this new issue.

This red 1d stamp was one of the six First Sidefaces, issued in 1874. Four years later they were supplemented by 2/- and 5/- values, which were the first postage stamps to be designed (by W.R. Bock) and entirely produced and printed in New Zealand.

Opposite: The 1873 ½d Newspaper stamp (top) showed a profile of Queen Victoria. The following year saw the issue of the First Sidefaces, which included a blue 6d stamp (bottom).

Watercolour artwork by A.E. Cousins for a 2½d design (unaccepted) for the Second Sideface issue, from 1891. Her Majesty is set in a lifebuoy/porthole frame, while steamships carry the 'home' mail to Britain.

The ½d value, designed by F.W. Sears, in the Second Sidefaces of 1882. This set of 10 'postage and revenue' stamps could be used for the payment of both postage and small revenue charges.

N.Z
POSTAGE & REVENUE
NEW ZEALAND
TWOPENCE
2½d
HALFPENNY

POSTAGE & REVENUE
NEW ZEALAND
TWOPENCE
2½d
HALFPENNY

As presented on the 2½d stamp, Victoria was also 'enveloped in fog'—an effect blamed on indifferent die cutting—and appeared to be 'growing a moustache.' But the reverse sides of these stamps also came in for criticism on account of their lack of gum. In 1897 one disgruntled customer wondered if this defective 'adhesive mucilage' which caused stamps to drop off letters was intentional, enabling the authorities to charge double the deficit and, further, resell stamps that had come adrift in post boxes.

The Full Faces and First Sidefaces were not immediately replaced by the Second Sidefaces but lingered until the last of them were withdrawn in 1884. By that time the Full Face image of Victoria was some 47 years old, and stamps bearing her portrait had served New Zealand for 43 years. In 1898, just three years before she died, monochrome portraits of the queen were finally replaced, giving way to more colourful tributes to this colony's natural features and scenic attractions. Nevertheless, in 1912 a noted British postal historian would describe New Zealand's Full Face Queen as 'one of the most handsome stamp designs known to the philatelist.'

Watercolour design (unaccepted), by A.E. Cousins, for the Second Sidefaces, c. 1891. A rather grim Victoria is presented in three-quarter pose rather than sideface.

Opposite: Watercolour artwork (left), by A.E. Cousins, for the 2½d stamp (right) in the Second Sideface issue, from 1891. The stamp suffered from problems in production and was the subject of considerable criticism.

2 representative of New Zealand

the first pictorials

For the first 43 years, all New Zealand's stamps carried the head of Victoria. The sole exception was the 1891 Government Life Insurance stamp (pp. 148–150), which featured a lighthouse, although it did include the royal reference 'V.R.' By then several colonies and countries—including New South Wales—had moved from heads of monarchs and presidents to pictorial designs. In late 1894 the New Zealand Government decided likewise.

In March 1895 a notice in the *New Zealand Gazette* invited 'persons resident in the colony' to suggest designs for a new issue of 11 stamps, which were to be 'scenic and representative of New Zealand.' The submitted designs were required to be of the exact intended sizes, although enlargements could also be provided, and to be sent under cover of a nom-de-plume. Entries had to be in by 31 July 1896. The series of designs judged by the postmaster-general to be the best and second-best would be awarded prizes of £150 and £100 respectively.

Lake Taupo, New Zealand's largest lake, was featured on the 1d stamp in the First Pictorials of 1898. Four years later the same design, by J. Gaut of Wellington, was used for the slightly smaller 4d stamp in a second set of Pictorials.

NEW ZEALAND
POSTAGE & REVENUE
1D.
ONE PENNY
1D.

The huia, which became extinct around 1907, was selected for the 3d stamp in the original Pictorial set of 1898, while a slightly smaller version was used in the Redrawn Pictorials of 1907. It was designed by W.R. Bock.

The designs were considered by a 'Board of Experts,' which included the president of the New Zealand Academy of Fine Arts, the director of the Wellington Technical School, a lecturer from the Canterbury College School of Art and the Government Printer. Their decisions were made public in early September and (for 6d admission) the public could inspect an exhibition of all submitted designs, about 2000, at the Academy of Fine Arts, Wellington. The noms-de-plume included 'Arawa', Aotearoa', 'Maori' and 'Mahi'. The eponymous 'Practical' (W.R. Bock of Wellington) was the most successful. His three first and two second prizes (as well as two honorable mentions) entitled him to £59 prize money out of the total pool of £250. The initial restriction to designers resident in New Zealand was later dropped and two Australians performed particularly well, in particular E.T. Luke ('Progress') of Melbourne, who managed two first and three second prizes. J. Gaut ('Tongariro') of Wellington and H.W. Young ('Arawa') of Ponsonby, Auckland, also managed two firsts each.

Perhaps the most prolific entrant was A.E. Cousins ('Maori') of Wellington, who was awarded one first and one honorable mention. While his image of Aoraki/Mt Cook was singled out by Wellington's *Evening Post* newspaper, the accepted version of that theme was by H.W. Young. Cousins also submitted designs using the huia (the subject of an accepted design by Bock) and moa, and an exquisite rendering entitled 'Mt Egmont from Albert Road,' showing Taranaki's dominant landform and the gaunt remains of forest clearance. But while this series of stamps would include a view of the White Terraces, destroyed in the eruption of Mt Tarawera in 1886, perhaps the destruction of native bush by settlers was not considered a suitable subject.

This first set of Pictorials consisted of 13 designs, the original list of 11 having been extended with a ½d and a 9d. As it turned out, seven of the designs—including New Zealand's national bird, the kiwi — were the work of Australians, Messrs. Luke (4) and Howard (3). The plates for the new stamps were engraved in England by Waterlow and Sons, who also made the first printings. In early 1898 the London correspondent for the *Evening Post* was able to have a preview of completed specimens at the office of the New Zealand agent-general. He reported: 'The work has been done exquisitely, and no country will be able to boast a finer set of postage stamps than New Zealand.' He was particularly

As with the huia on the 3d stamp, the 1/- design (also by W.R. Bock), depicting the kea and kaka, appeared in two sets of Pictorials, in 1898 and 1907.

impressed by 'the light and shade in these little etchings of Mount Cook, Milford Haven [sic], Ruapehu etc.,' while the only stamp he did not approve of was that of the kiwi.

The stamps went on sale on 4 April 1898 and overseas response was extremely favourable. The *London Philatelist* regarded them as 'one of the most perfect sets ... in use throughout the British Empire', while the *Pall Mall Magazine* described them as 'a picture gallery in miniature' which 'combines advertisement with an artistic design' and suggests that 'in mountain scenery New Zealand is a serious rival of Norway.' But not everyone was so impressed back home. In 1899 a politician reportedly complained about the Premier's 'erasing from the postage stamps of the colony the figure of the Queen's head', and pleaded 'for the restoration of same.'

The Pictorials covered scenery (nine stamps) and birds (three stamps), while one particularly cluttered design included tree ferns, cabbage trees, a war canoe and crown (p. 33). Of the two additions to the original list, the lowest denomination—½d—depicted New Zealand's highest peak, Aoraki/Mt Cook, while the 9d was of the Pink Terraces at Rotomahana, which, like the White Terraces on the 4d stamp, had been destroyed in the eruption of Mt Tarawera just 12 years previously. While Milford Sound (with Mitre Peak) and Mt Cook may have been the most recognisable of the (surviving) landscape views, perhaps the best-known image was that of Lake Wakatipu, which was distinguished by its famous misspelling as 'Wakitipu'.

On 7 March 1900 five of the original Pictorials reappeared in different colours, sizes and denominations. They were followed 11 months later by an entirely new design which was not inspired by local scenery but events in another continent. On 11 October 1899 the British Government accepted New Zealand's offer of trained troops to assist with the worsening situation in South Africa. This was the first force of men to be raised in this country and dispatched abroad to represent it in combat. The first of 10 contingents sailed from Wellington on 21 October, and the country swelled with pride. This willing assistance to the motherland was surely evidence of the young colony's growing maturity and sense of responsibility.

Following the Relief of Mafeking on 17 May 1900, the Boers appeared to be in retreat, but the war was far from over. In late November Lord Kitchener took over as Commander-in-Chief of the British forces. Soon

The 2½d stamp (top) in the 1898 Pictorials was designed by E.T. Luke and depicted Lake Wakatipu, the second-largest lake in the South Island. Its first printing was distinguished by the famous spelling mistake: 'Wakitipu'. The 2/- stamp, also designed by E.T. Luke, showcased Mitre Peak (on the right) at Milford Sound, the well-known fiord on the south-western coastline of the South Island.

The original line art for the patriotic South African (Boer) War stamp included in the 1900 Pictorials. It was designed by Scottish-born Wellington artist James Nairn and appeared in military khaki colour when printed.

NEW ZEALAND
1½ D
THE EMPIRES CALL
POSTAGE & REVENUE

afterwards, New Zealand issued a South African (Boer) War stamp, designed by Scottish-born artist James Nairn. He had come to New Zealand in 1880 and was an influential teacher, painting in an impressionistic manner and encouraging a *plein-air* approach. Unfortunately his ideas did not necessarily translate into a successful postage stamp. His war design was disadvantaged by an excess of patriotic devices, from the catch-cry 'The Empire's Call' and a winged female figure sounding a bugle to the New Zealand flag, officers and troops and, among other things, Maori carving and an army camp. Appropriately, the stamps were printed in khaki, the colour of military uniforms.

The Pink and White Terraces were destroyed with the eruption of Mt Tarawera in 1886. Twelve years later the White Terraces were shown on the 4d stamp (designed by E. Howard) in the original Pictorial set, while the Pink Terraces were remembered on the 9d stamp, designed by W.R. Bock.

While New Zealand waited anxiously for news from the war in South Africa, it learned of the death of Queen Victoria on 22 January 1901. Auckland marked the event with the 'slow and mournful' ringing of bells tolling 82 times—one for each year of Her late Majesty's life. Meanwhile, the *Evening Post* reported that a Wellington firm of cabinetmakers and upholsters had placed a black band around postage stamps bearing the late queen on all their outgoing mail.

Just as the original pictorial set had undergone several changes, in 1907 the need to replace printing plates was an opportunity to reduce the size of three denominations. And, as in 1900, a new—albeit six-year-old—design, the 1901 Penny Universal, was spruced up and included. These Redrawn Pictorials and other earlier ones were in use until replaced in 1909 by designs that returned to an earlier theme, the monarch's head. The Pictorials had been a popular departure at the time, although many of their central images were overwhelmed by excessively decorative borders. By today's standards they seem rather tentative celebrations of New Zealand's distinctive features. Nevertheless, they reflected the spirit of the times and make a striking comparison with the treatment of similar subjects a century or so later.

For the 8d stamp in the original 1898 Pictorials, designer E. Howard employed number-eight ingenuity to frame vignettes of the British crown and a Maori canoe. Tree ferns (left) and cabbage trees (right) complete the picture.

3 into the penny zone

universal postage

On 1 January 1901, the arrival of a new century was marked in Wellington by the launch of a new postage stamp. That event was an invitation-only official function, although the large crowd of revellers outside the General Post Office was soon aware that postal history was about to be made.

A quarter of an hour before midnight and, as the *Evening Post* put it, the 'expiration' of the old year, images of three postage stamps—1d, 2d and 2½d—which were about to become redundant, were projected on a screen by means of lantern slides. Then, on the first stroke of midnight, a rocket was fired from the parapet of the GPO and a 'bomb' burst overhead. On the last stroke of the hour the building 'flashed into a blaze of light' and the images of the 'old' stamps were then replaced by projections of a new stamp, the Royal Arms and a portrait of Queen Victoria painted by James Nairn, who had been responsible for the design of New Zealand's South African (Boer) War stamp, which was issued just three weeks earlier.

In her left hand Zealandia holds a caduceus, a herald's staff entwined by serpents and surmounted by wings. It represents the Roman god Mercury, messenger of the gods and, in the 19th century, a symbol of the postal service. As a representation of New Zealand, Zealandia made her postal debut in 1901, on this design by Guido Bach.

NEW ZEALAND
UNIVERSAL POSTAGE
ONE PENNY

The original 1901 Penny Universal stamp subsequently underwent various modifications and reprintings, including the 1907 Dominion version, which was also overprinted for official uses.

There were fireworks and illuminations in red, white and blue provided by 623 lamps. The overall effect was as if 'some Eastern palace had been set down on the shore of the Southern Sea.' Meanwhile, inside the GPO a meeting of the Executive Council of Government approved regulations that brought into force a new system of universal penny postage. The Postmaster-General, Joseph Ward, was then presented with a shield bearing a facsimile of the new penny stamp, which had been engraved in pure gold by W.R. Bock. The cost of this had been borne by Post and Telegraph staff, whose individual contributions were—appropriately—limited to one penny. In reply Ward noted the importance of the occasion and that New Zealand was the first country to adopt the universal penny post. He had been 'labouring incessantly' since 1891 to bring about this 'great reform' and was able to announce that New Zealanders could now send letters for 1d to the United Kingdom, as well as some 70 other countries and British possessions and protectorates, from Aden to Zanzibar. He regretted that because Australia was awaiting the establishment of the Federal Government it was not yet able to join the system, and so postage across the Tasman would be 2d. Prior to the introduction of universal penny postage the rate to the United Kingdom had been 2½d per half ounce, while a number of foreign countries also agreed to deliver penny letters that were posted from New Zealand.

In 1907 the now six-year-old Penny Universal stamp was modified to acknowledge New Zealand's new dominion status, and issued along with redrawn versions of three of the original 1898 Pictorials.

There was a keen demand for the stamps following their release on 1 January. By mid-morning Christchurch's whole supply of 7200 had been sold out and large crowds were reportedly turned away from the Post Office. In Wellington the first stamp was bought by Malcolm Ross, the New Zealand correspondent for *The Times*. He put it to good use, explaining in his report to London: 'The penny stamp that conveys this letter over 13,000 miles of land and sea is worth preserving, because of its historic interest.' His account, published exactly two months later, described how the first supply of 100,000 stamps was quickly sold out, and by the end of the first day stamps were changing hands privately for 1/- each. Fortunately, a further shipment arrived from England the following day, with another million expected shortly.

Originally Thomas De La Rue & Co. of London had been approached to both design and supply the printed stamps. But when they were unable to guarantee delivery, the contract went to Waterlow & Sons, who had engraved and printed New Zealand's first pictorial issue of 1898. The President of the Royal Academy and popular painter of historical subjects, Sir Edward Poynter, had agreed to design the stamp, but he became 'indisposed'. The printers then commissioned Guido Bach, an Austrian-born artist who moved to London in 1862. Required to show a female figure symbolic of New Zealand, Bach placed Zealandia in front of a globe and with a mailboat passing Mt Taranaki/Egmont in the background. Zealandia had made her first appearance some four decades earlier, as the title of a guide book for emigrants to the antipodes: *New Zealand or Zealandia, The Britain of the South Seas*. The idea of Britannia's daughter in the southern colony caught on, particularly with composers of patriotic verse, while cartoonists also made much of the symbolic figure in a classical garb. At the close of the 19th century, the independent-minded Zealandia declined the invitation to join the federation of Australian states and was a natural choice to grace this country's pioneering universal penny postage stamp. Then in 1911 she became a supporter—a 'female figure proper' in heraldic terminology—on this country's coat of arms, while modifications made in 1956 gave her a more modern hairstyle and gown.

The Penny Universal stamp was overprinted to coincide with the opening of the Auckland Exhibition, held in the domain in 1913-14. These stamps were only sold at the Exhibition, which included a Palace of Industries and Wonderland fun fair.

In 1910 Zealandia's domain extended to Victoria Land, a region of Antarctica discovered in 1841. The 1909 1d Dominion Universal Postage stamp was overprinted for use by Captain R.F. Scott's Antarctic expedition of 1910–1913.

The inauguration of the penny postage system proved extremely popular, stimulating a 30 percent increase in the number of letters posted in New Zealand in the second week of January 1901. The total number of such items handled during that period was 786,351, compared to 605,668 in the corresponding week of the previous year. The district experiencing the greatest increase was Christchurch, with a massive 50 percent, in contrast to the letter-writers of New Plymouth, who managed only a 13 percent increase in their mail.

When establishing penny postage, Joseph Ward correctly anticipated it would initially result in a loss of revenue for the Postal Department. But the deficit was recovered in less than two years, a result of New Zealanders taking advantage of the reduced postage to send more mail. While the system proved popular, the stamp itself had its detractors. One critic likened Zealandia to a schoolteacher giving a geography lesson, but the most memorable perspective was offered by Denis Glover in the 1966 *Encyclopaedia of New Zealand*: 'From 1901 till 1909, in a well-washed red, her figure was daily battered by the cancellation mark of every post office in the land. Zealandia has suffered a sea change. She now stands on the end of a wharf, leaning against a murky globe. The caduceus shows signs of weighing heavy, and her right hand rests unsteadily on the foremast of a proud steamer tossing in mid-Tasman. She has lost her hat, and her tresses are wildly windswept. There is a slight glaze to her eye: she looks dissolute. Against the gale her nightie is reinforced by a nether Kaiapoi rug. It is cold, and there's not a sailor in sight.'

In 1911 Joseph Ward was able to report that Australia had finally accepted the universal postage system, and had now 'come into the penny zone.' He knew of no better method to bring 'the men and women in the backblocks into touch with their friends and relations in other parts of the world' than 'the magnificent system of penny postage.' New Zealanders were certainly taking advantage of it; in 1912 it was claimed they had attained the highest position in the Universal Postal Union in terms of the number of items posted per head of population. This country led the field with 139 items, followed by Britain (111) and Germany (100).

Since its debut, New Zealand's penny stamp had enjoyed several reappearances. A clearer version was included in the Redrawn Pictorials of 1907, and two years later it was further modified to acknowledge the colony's transition to a dominion. As with the Full Face Queens, it appeared in a wide range of varieties, a result of different plates, papers and perforations. Zealandia continued to provide penny postage until 1926, when she was finally retired after a record quarter of a century of service.

New Zealand's postal rates increased during the First World War, but penny postage was restored in 1923. This stamp, designed by W.R. Bock and showing an oddly drawn outline map of the country, was issued to mark the event. For a period it existed alongside the original Penny Universal stamp, from which it had borrowed several design elements.

4 for the benefit of the empire

1906 exhibition

The arrival of the Arawa canoe in Aotearoa/New Zealand, as interpreted by Louis J. Steele. This ½d stamp was the lowest denomination in the set marking the 1906-07 New Zealand International Exhibition of Arts and Industries in Christchurch.

The 1851 Great Exhibition at London's Crystal Palace was conceived by Prince Albert, Queen Victoria's husband, and was the first of a series of massive international displays of manufactures and arts. New Zealand was represented at the event and 14 years later mounted the first such exhibition of its own, in Dunedin. Others followed in the main centres at regular intervals, among them the 1906-07 New Zealand International Exhibition of Arts and Industries in Christchurch. It was the country's largest such undertaking to date and further distinguished by an issue of postage stamps.

The exhibition was not as international as its name suggested. While there were some exhibits by individual foreign companies, the nations of Europe were not officially represented and there was nothing from the United States. Nevertheless, the display of local manufacturers demonstrated New Zealand's 'independence of foreign competitors' and gave 'a fine illustration of the vast resources and enterprises of the great Empire to which we belong.'

NEW ZEALAND
POSTAGE & REVENUE
½D
HALFPENNY
TE ARAWA
COMMEMORATIVE SERIES OF 1906

In fact, it was claimed the exhibition amply demonstrated that there was nothing that was needed in 'the home, the field, or the workshop' that could not be supplied by New Zealand or the 'Mother and sister states of the Empire.' The quality of British workmanship was 'in evidence on every hand,' and New Zealand visitors could feel well satisfied with goods made 'under the glimmer of the Southern Cross.' Provincial displays testified to the 'wonderful potentialities and prosperity' of the colony, while those by government departments were a record of positive progress. The Prisons Department exhibit, for example, illustrated what went on in the colony's 'reformatories'. A highlight of the exhibition was the British court, where the art—a 'show of masterpieces rare and rich'—was said to be the finest ever sent from England.

The exhibition was located in Hagley Park, and in addition to displays of art and industry it offered daily entertainment by an orchestra, haka performances in a Maori village and the sideshows of 'Wonderland'. The grand closing ceremony, on 15 April, was likened to 'the passing of a great entity into a memory. The curtain is down, the players are going home, but the record of their performance will long remain.' The event had attracted a total attendance of 1,970,000, a little over twice the total population of the country at the time. It was a remarkable turnout, but the main aim of the exhibition was to 'give a practical lesson on New Zealand for the benefit of the Empire, and a practical lesson on the Empire for the benefit of New Zealand.'

The stamp designs selected to mark the exhibition also gave a practical lesson on New Zealand history. While earlier Pictorial issues had depicted aspects of the geographical past (as in the recently destroyed Pink and White Terraces) and a contemporary event (the South African War), this 1906 set was the first to address human settlement. They were designed by English-born artist Louis J. Steele, who arrived in Auckland in 1886 and soon established a reputation for painted portraits. His sitters included such notables as John Logan Campbell and George Grey, as well as a series of successful racehorses. He also specialised in historical subjects, and his designs for the 1906 stamps covered aspects of the colony's development, from the arrival of its first settlers from Polynesia to its annexation by Great Britain in 1840.

Steele was a leading member of a group of late 19th-century New Zealand artists interested in the life and traditions of the ancient Maori. This local branch of history painting was concerned with recording aspects of the vanishing past and reflected New Zealand's growing sense of independence and a distinct national identity. The colony would graduate to dominion status in 1907, and its need for a sense of history prior to its few decades of organised settlement from Europe was now provided by the world of the Maori.

Louis J. Steele's original designs for his Christchurch Exhibition stamps of 1906 consisted of same-sized watercolours and enlarged versions of the main image.

Opposite: The printed version of the Landing of Cook at Poverty Bay, on 8 October 1769. This historic encounter is set within a highly decorative border.

Steele's four postal designs were in ascending chronological order and began, on the ½d stamp, with the arrival of the Arawa canoe off Cape Runaway, at the north-eastern end of the Bay of Plenty (p. 43). He had previously painted images of canoes, including his 1890 collaboration with fellow Auckland artist Kennett Watkins, *The Explosion of the Boyd*. This interpretation of the massacre in Whangaroa Harbour in 1809 was hardly a suitable subject for a stamp, and neither was his later (1916) *The Launching of a Maori Canoe*, which included a human sacrifice. But it was another of Steele's collaborations, with his former pupil Charles F. Goldie, that in 1898

NEW ZEALAND
POSTAGE & REVENUE
3
THREEPENCE
LANDING OF COOK
COMMEMORATIVE SERIES OF 1906

had produced this country's best-known historical painting, *The Arrival of the Maoris in New Zealand*. This highly detailed but ethnologically inaccurate depiction of emaciated east Polynesian voyagers making landfall in Aotearoa reflected the prevailing European notions of a Great Fleet.

From Polynesian origins Maori culture evolved to include a rich tradition of woodcarving. Steele made field trips around the North Island, sketching such aspects of Maori life and amassing a personal collection of artefacts. Further, he acknowledged the achievements of Maori art on his 1d design, which featured the carving of a canoe prow. This ancient tradition would quickly adapt to metal tools resulting from contact from Europe, and Steele's 3d stamp recorded the landing of Captain Cook, at Poverty Bay, on 8 October 1769. This was another theme familiar to Steele, as seen in his 1890 painting (also with Kennett Watkins) *Arrival of Captain Cook; An incident in the Bay of Islands 29 November 1769*. Earlier, Cook had been acknowledged indirectly with two Pictorial stamps featuring the eponymous mountain, but Steele's stamp design was the first in this country to feature the great navigator himself.

Nineteen years after the Christchurch Exhibition, the 1925-26 New Zealand and South Seas Exhibition was held in Dunedin. It was that city's third such event (following others in 1865 and 1889-90), and was the subject of a set of three stamps designed by H. Linley Richardson.

The publication in Europe of Cook's voyages stimulated interest in New Zealand. Reluctant at first, the British Government was eventually forced to take action and so dispatched William Hobson to the Bay of Islands. As lieutenant-governor he proclaimed the sovereignty of Queen Victoria over New Zealand, and the raising of the flagstaff was the subject of the 6d stamp in the 1906 series.

Steele's history paintings were highly popular, but his images did not translate so happily to postage stamp scale and were further disadvantaged by indifferent printing. And as with certain earlier Pictorial stamps, the designs were overwhelmed by heavy borders. But perhaps the most significant feature of this series was the 1d stamp, which was reprinted in vermilion when claret was found unsatisfactory. A small number of the claret originals was issued by mistake and are now among the rarest of all New Zealand's stamps.

H. Linley Richardson's designs for the 1925-26 Dunedin Exhibition stamps were distinguished by their borders consisting of Maori taniko (weaving) patterns. Another startling innovation was the pair of grimacing figures in the top corners.

5 from colony to dominion

Edward VII

'Round the world, now flashing along the mighty ocean's measureless depths, now traversing with lightning rapidity vast continents, rushed forth the record of a nation's bereavement. Each centre sent it tearing on its tireless way through countless branches and ramifications, till every remote town and hamlet in the Empire knew that Victoria was no more.' With barely contained enthusiasm for what was then the latest word in communication technology, the *New Zealand Illustrated Magazine* reported how this country, along with the rest of the empire, had learned of the death of Queen Victoria on 21 January 1901.

Victoria had reigned for five months short of 64 years. She was succeeded by her eldest son, the Prince of Wales, who was then aged nearly 60 and had acquired a reputation as a playboy. The *Observer* noted that as King Edward VII he faced a stern challenge for 'no British monarch was ever before so universally loved by her people as was Queen Victoria.' On occasions the

The 6d stamp, one of nine depicting Edward VII, king over what was now the Dominion of New Zealand. They were designed by W.R. Royle & Sons, England, and issued in November 1909.

DOMINION OF
NEW ZEALAND
6d.
6d.
POSTAGE
REVENUE
SIX PENCE

The 2d stamp was part of the set issued in 1909, over eight years after the proclamation of Edward VII as king.

prince's conduct had 'rather jarred upon the popular sense of propriety' but in spite of 'all his foibles' he remained popular. Now, having presumably 'completely outgrown his youthful follies,' he could bring to his next duty a 'mature judgment [and] a ripe knowledge of men and things.' But he had to wait before his image appeared on New Zealand postage stamps, and by the time it did this most distant part of his empire had undergone a change of status.

On 28 January 1901 the New Zealand Government issued instructions relating to the proclamation of the new king. Businesses were required to close from 11 to 1 o'clock, and flags were to be hoisted 'mast high'. In Nelson a 21-gun royal salute was fired, and a large crowd gathered in Trafalgar Street. The chief postmaster then handed the mayor a telegraphed copy of the proclamation, which he read from the steps of Christ Church Cathedral. Under the names of the governor (Lord Ranfurly), premier (Richard Seddon) and members of the executive council, it proclaimed Edward VII 'King of the United Kingdom of Great Britain and Ireland, Defender of the Faith, Emperor of India, and Supreme Lord in and over the Colony of New Zealand and its dependencies.' Then followed three cheers for the new king, accompanied by the pealing of church and fire bells, and with the singing of 'God Save the King' the proceedings were complete.

At this time New Zealand was well-served by existing postage stamps. The popularity of the earlier Pictorial issues, as well as the appearance of the Penny Universal postage stamp less than a month prior to the death of Victoria, meant there was no pressure to produce a stamp depicting Edward VII. But in mid-1906 it was decided to issue such a set, which would also retain the universal penny postage design. The latter now underwent a number of modifications, the most significant being acknowledgement of New Zealand's graduation from a colony to a dominion on 26 September 1907. A public holiday was declared and Dominion Night saw crowds surging into city centres to enjoy the festivities. In Wellington the lights 'drew the moths in myriads.' People made their way to the Government Buildings to watch the start of a torchlight procession, of veterans, troops, cadets, the fire brigade and various bands—in all 'a blaze of light and a blare of sound.' The Governor, Lord Plunket, explained that as a dominion, New Zealand now took 'a seat among the rising nations of

The 1909 Edward VII stamps presented the king in a three-quarter left-facing pose, similar to that given to Victoria on the Full Face Queens from 1855.

The Edward VII stamps of 1909 were similar, the only major change to the set being the replacement of the 4d orange by the 4d yellow, to assist legibility.

our Empire' and he believed it would encourage the spirit of nationalism essential for achieving self-reliance. The new status was really little more than a change of name, although it was good for business, stimulating a flurry of products—including a Wellington newspaper—proudly bearing the name *Dominion*. Before long the ex-colony would acquire another sign of maturity, in the form of its own official coat of arms. This was granted in 1911 and featured Zealandia, who had already given over a decade's service to local stamps and would reappear as part of another issue in 1931.

New Zealand's Edward VII stamps were issued in November 1909, nearly nine years after he had assumed the throne. They were designed by the English company W. R. Royle & Sons, and there were eight denominations, from ½d to 1/-, in addition to the modified 1901 Penny Universal stamp. With the exception of the latter they showed a left-facing three-quarter portrait of the bemedalled and fashionably heavily bearded king, with a superimposed crown. The portrait on the ½d stamp differed slightly from the others and, as well as colour, there were also slight variations in backgrounds and the borders enclosing the denominations. Together, they were the only set of stamps to be emblazoned 'Dominion of New Zealand.'

King Edward VII reigned for a little over nine years and three months, dying on 6 May 1910 after a series of bronchial and heart attacks. Once again, the post offices of New Zealand played a pivotal role in advising citizens of the appropriate observance. Telegrams were sent by the government to all mayors, chairmen of local bodies and ministers of religion to encourage a 'uniformity of action in connection with the lamentable death of our late beloved Sovereign.' It requested that women and girls wear a black ribbon on the right arm above the elbow, while men wear one on their coat lapel. Flags on public buildings were to be at half mast, with a black streamer flying a foot above each. On the day of the funeral, usual train services would be maintained, but at an appointed time all trains would simultaneously be at a standstill throughout the country for 15 minutes.

Edward VII died just six months after his image appeared on this country's stamps. However, it would continue to be associated with our mail for several more years, until superseded by those honouring his son, George V.

Portraits of Edward VII occupied eight values in the 1909 issue, while the 1d was a redrawn version of the universal postage stamp of 1901.

6 admiral of the fleet

George V

Following George V's ascension to the throne, on 6 May 1910, the *Evening Post* patriotically reported that 'many hundreds of thousands' of New Zealanders had either already met or taken part in public functions attended by His Highness. This was a result of his visit here nine years earlier, in July 1901 as the Duke of Cornwall and York, when he and the Duchess brought Britain's thanks for this country's support during the war in South Africa. Over 16 days the royal pair made a 'triumphant progress through the Dominion', their numerous duties including attending a large Maori gathering in Rotorua and laying the foundation stone for the Wellington Town Hall.

The duke became King George V, and the coronation took place on 22 June 1911. The occasion was marked in Wellington by warships in the harbour being decorated 'rainbow fashion … from stem to stern' and firing royal salutes at noon, while there were also the obligatory illuminations on government buildings and a torch-light procession. Summery weather

This 1d George V Admiral stamp of 1926, designed by H. Linley Richardson, replaced both the 1923 1d Map stamp and the long-serving 1901 universal postage stamp.

POSTAGE AND REVENUE
1D
1D
NEW ZEALAND

Original line drawing by H. Linley Richardson for the 2/- George V Admiral stamp issued in 1926. The design included Maori taniko patterns on either side and the four stars of the Southern Cross.

favoured a ceremony on Napier's Marine Parade, but heavy rain caused celebrations to be held indoors in Westport. In Feilding the district high school presented a miniature coronation pageant.

New Zealand had a new king, but it also still had an ample supply of stamps bearing the image of the previous monarch, Edward VII. When this country's Postmaster General, Joseph Ward, was in London in May 1911 he suggested a new set was imminent, remarking that the portrait of George V would be a credit to New Zealand's Postal Department. He also stated that he believed great care was needed in the design of postage stamps, and that it was undesirable to change them too frequently—which may explain why another four years elapsed before the George V stamps appeared.

As well as appearing on stamps, George V collected them. This enthusiastic philatelist also took a keen interest in aspects of their design and encouraged consistency when it came to depicting the royal head. In late 1911 the *London Telegraph* reported that the design of New Zealand's new George V issue would be placed in the hands of British sculptor Bertram Mackennal, who had been responsible for that country's recent British coinage. It also reported that the design would depart from previous practice by expressing the denominations in numerals only instead of either words or a combination of both. But Mackennal did not accept the commission and the design became the responsibility of H. Linley Richardson, an English-born artist and teacher who had come to New Zealand in 1908.

Richardson taught life drawing at Wellington Technical School, while also painting and doing illustration work. He produced a large number of portraits, including those of two Victoria Cross winners for the Dominion Museum in 1920 and of Liberal Member of Parliament Sir James Carroll in 1926. He also did portraits of himself and members of his family in domestic situations, an unusual subject for the time. His best-known painting is *Mrs Thornley of Titahi Bay*, in 1931-32, depicting the elderly proprietor of a hotel north of Wellington where the Richardsons spent their holidays.

This stamp commission required Richardson to produce a portrait on a miniature scale. His design was first issued on 30 July 1915, and the left-facing profile of George V echoed the Penny Black of 1840. Unlike the earlier 1909 Edward VII issue there was now no reference to dominion status; the

In the manner of the Penny Black of 86 years earlier, H. Linley Richardson presented George V in a left-facing profile.

H. Linley Richardson's 1925 George V stamps remained in service until 1935. There were 13 different denominations, from ½d to 1/-, but no 1d until the Admiral set of 1926.

4½D 4½D
POSTAGE & REVENUE
NEW ZEALAND

5D 5D
POSTAGE & REVENUE
NEW ZEALAND

6D 6D
POSTAGE & REVENUE
NEW ZEALAND

7½D 7½D
POSTAGE & REVENUE
NEW ZEALAND

8D 8D
POSTAGE & REVENUE
NEW ZEALAND

8D 8D
POSTAGE & REVENUE
NEW ZEALAND

9D 9D
POSTAGE & REVENUE
NEW ZEALAND

1S 1S
POSTAGE & REVENUE
NEW ZEALAND

country of origin reverted to simply 'New Zealand'. But there was a strong local reference, for this stamp was the first to include a Maori design, adapted from a traditional rafter pattern. In addition, the four stars of the Southern Cross were placed in the two lower corners. It was a well-balanced design, for the king was not overwhelmed by the surrounding border or other devices. A London publication considered it 'striking', and was confident it would 'meet with the general approval of philatelists.' The interest of collectors was no doubt further heightened by the many variations that followed, a result of different printing methods, overprintings and changes of colour. As if to compensate for the initial four-year delay, these stamps remained in use until 1935 and appeared in a total of 13 different denominations, from ½d to 1/-. However, there was no need for a George V 1d stamp, because of the existing universal postage design, which had served, subject to changes, since 1901.

In 1925 Richardson received two more stamp commissions. The first, marking the 1925-26 New Zealand and South Seas Exhibition in Dunedin, made greater use of a Maori decorative border. For the second commission, resulting from the growing demand for higher denomination 2/- and 3/- stamps, Richardson undertook another design depicting George V. Viscount Jellicoe, commander of the British fleet at the Battle of Jutland in 1916, was now Governor-General of New Zealand, so it was decided that the king should be depicted in the uniform of an admiral. As before he was shown in strict profile, left-facing and framed by a Maori border design. And because by now the Post Office finally needed a new 1d stamp, Richardson also provided another smaller design. The king was shown in the uniform of a field marshal, the highest military rank in the British Army, and one traditionally taken by the monarchy. His cocked hat, now with a drooping plume, broke the border and required the central crown to be replaced by a symmetrical pair in the upper corners, while the 1d denominations were relocated to the side panels. These three so-called Admiral stamps were issued in July 1926 and were in use until New Zealand's next Pictorial set appeared in 1935.

Richardson's latest stamp design had the unusual distinction of being the subject of comment in Parliament. On 23 July 1926, a fortnight after their issue, Auckland East MP John A. Lee referred to a recent article in the *Auckland Star* which claimed the new stamps made His Majesty 'look like a Dutch doll.' Lee regarded stamps as 'a unique opportunity of advertising the country', and felt it a pity if it was going to produce a stamp that both failed in this duty and which 'practically cartooned His Majesty.' Lee admitted he hadn't actually seen the stamp in question, but on the basis of the article was convinced that it was 'not a credit to New Zealand.'

The green ½d , the lowest denomination in the George V issue of 1915 designed by H. Linley Richardson.

7 purely postal purposes

victory 1920

On 5 August 1914 New Zealand joined Britain in declaring war on Germany, following that country's invasion of Belgium. Unfolding events led the British Foreign Secretary to observe, famously: 'The lamps are going out all over Europe; we shall not see them lit again in our lifetime.' The New Zealand Government promptly authorised the formation of an Expeditionary Force, and such was local enthusiasm for the 'Great Adventure' that within a day more than 3000 Aucklanders had volunteered to serve. Altogether 124,111 New Zealand males—just over half of those eligible—were called up, and over 103,000 from this country served overseas. They suffered the highest casualty rate in the empire, with 16,554 making the ultimate sacrifice and nearly 50,000 being wounded either in or as a result of the war.

Eleven months after the declaration of war, New Zealand issued its first set of stamps to show George V. They were on sale for the duration of the hostilities, and the ½d value was overprinted 'War Stamp' to

A female figure and a British lion proclaim victory in 1920.

VICTORY STAMP
POSTAGE & REVENUE
1d
NEW ZEALAND

VICTORY STAMP
POSTAGE & REVENUE
1d
NEW ZEALAND

A female personification of Victory rests against a recumbent lion, and wears and holds wreaths of laurel leaves. The original artwork is by English printers Thomas de la Rue, and the 1920 New Zealand ½d Victory stamp is shown opposite.

½d
NEW ZEALAND VICTORY STAMP
½d
1914
POSTAGE & REVENUE
1919

acknowledge a necessary increase in the cost of postage. The king, who had served in the Royal Navy, was a first cousin of the German Kaiser Wilhelm I, and in July 1917 he responded to anti-German sentiment by changing the name of the British Royal house from Saxe-Coburg-Gotha to Windsor.

Although New Zealand had produced a themed stamp during the hostilities in South Africa in 1900, it did not do so for the First World War. The disastrous campaign at Gallipoli in 1915 became a subject much later, but it was peace rather than action that would stimulate this country's next stamps, which were suggested soon after the cessation of hostilities on 1 November 1918.

The war had interrupted the production of postage stamps, but a return to normality prompted a number of colonies, including New Zealand, to plan new issues. The *Manchester Guardian*, which had earlier been extremely complimentary about New Zealand's George V stamps, now reported that it produced the empire's first Victory stamps, although its seems Jamaica had already issued—and withdrawn—such a set. New Zealand's designs were provided by English printers Thomas de la Rue and selected by Sir Joseph Ward when he was in London early in 1919. A British stamp magazine had suggested New Zealand was taking advantage of collectors by producing new issues, but Postmaster-General (and later Prime Minister) Gordon

A victorious lion rests, while the rising sun represents the dawn of peace. The original artwork by English printers Thomas de la Rue, and the 1920 New Zealand 3d Victory stamp.

Coates stated that his department's sole concern was stamps 'for purely postal purposes.' He pointed out that the new Victory series would be in use alongside regular postage stamps, on sale for a limited period and valid only for inland use. In response to accusations of over-production, Coates said New Zealand was not planning a new general issue. In fact, one did not appear for another 16 years, until 1935.

An immediate rush was reported in Wellington when New Zealand's Victory series went on sale on 27 January 1920. In the opinion of *The Times* they were 'one of the most effective stamp issues that have been seen for some time.' Not surprisingly for a set of stamps designed in England and commemorating Allied success, they were heavy in imperial symbolism. The lion, representing the victorious British Empire, appeared on four of the stamps, and was derived from the four huge sculptures designed for the base of Nelson's Column in Trafalgar Square by the painter Edwin Landseer. The *Manchester Guardian* suggested the lion's previously rare appearances on British stamps was a result of criticism of an 'underfed specimen' on the first of the King George V stamps in 1912 and 1913. In contrast, New Zealand's Victory stamps demonstrated that 'very imposing use' could be made of the king of the jungle. Four years later Britain made amends, presenting a much more impressive and well-nourished lion on its British Empire Exhibition stamps.

The angel of peace accompanied by a child representing progress on the 6d 1920 Victory stamp.

A traditional chief represented the contribution made by the Maori of New Zealand during the recent war, on the 1½d Victory stamp. The original wash drawing and the printed stamp (opposite).

Female allegorical figures were also popular with the new New Zealand series. The ½d stamp showed Peace gracefully resting on what was described as a 'recumbent' (or 'couchant', in heraldic terms) lion. On the 1d (red, as required by the Postal Union), Victory stood beside a lion and held a 'graceful spray,' while the 6d stamp depicted an Angel of Peace with outstretched wings and a small child, as Progress, bearing a palm. The boldest (3d) design was of a lion resting after victory against a background of the rising sun, representing a new dawn.

Recognisable New Zealand imagery was generally subservient to the theme of empire, but the notable exception was the 1½d stamp, which acknowledged the contribution made by Maori in the recent war. Although there was resistance to supporting the British Crown from Maori communities which had suffered land confiscations in the 19th century, some 2000 individuals served, as part of Native Contingent (at Gallipoli) and the Pioneer Battalion (in Egypt and France). The stamp showed a traditional Maori chief, with tattooed face, huia feathers in his hair and an ear pendant of shark teeth. Rather than a warrior who had fought in the recent so-called Great War, it was a chief of yesteryear and reminiscent of the subjects then being painted by Charles F. Goldie and, earlier, Gottfried Lindauer. The chief's head was balanced by carvings and a background of fern, which one local commentator noted was not in fact a known New Zealand species. Not surprisingly, the highest denomination (1/-) in the set depicted a three-quarter portrait of George V in uniform, flanked by lions' heads, and with a small Maori pa in the upper corners.

On 3 May 1919, five months after the Armistice, New Zealanders had taken part in Dominion Troops' Day in London, watched by a large crowd which included Winston Churchill and the king and queen. According to *The Times*, the New Zealand contingent consisted of 'tall, graceful men' who marched with 'freedom and yet with a kind of dignified reserve.' These service personnel returned home to a succession of peace celebrations, which included the Victory stamps. The League of Nations had been formed a fortnight earlier and Joseph Ward was confident this organisation would guarantee that there would be no more wars for 'at least 50 or 100 years.'

8 for children in need

early health stamps

In 1929 New Zealand launched a postal innovation that became an annual institution. It had its origins in Denmark when a mail clerk, Einar Holboell, suggested Christmas seals as a means of raising funds for a hospital for children suffering from tuberculosis. The scheme began in 1904 and three years later spread to the United States. In 1926 Kirstine Nielsen, who had emigrated from Denmark to New Zealand, suggested to the Norsewood branch of the Country Women's Institute that the system be adopted in this country. It was accepted by the Post and Telegraph Department, with the initial plan for a 1d stamp which could be affixed voluntarily to letters and supplement the ordinary postage stamp.

Children's health camps were the result of an initiative by Dr Elizabeth Gunn, a captain in the New Zealand Medical Corps during the First World War. She determined to do something about the problem of child

Viewed through a keyhole, a happy child represents the key to health on this 1935 stamp, designed by S. Hall and the New Zealand Post and Telegraph Department, Wellington. A typical New Zealand beach scene is combined with a rising sun and side panels of geometrical Maori motifs.

POSTAGE HEALTH
1D 1D
NEW ZEALAND
POSTAGE HEALTH
1D 1D
NEW ZEALAND

This Help Promote Health stamp, designed by Leonard C. Mitchell and the Government Printer, Wellington, was issued in 1930. The same design, but with the slogan 'Help Stamp Out Tuberculosis', was used the previous year for New Zealand's first Health stamp.

malnutrition, and in 1919 she obtained the use of a farm at Turakina, near Whanganui, to set up a camp for children in need. Government departments and local organisations provided food and equipment, and 55 children spent some three weeks under canvas. This was the first of what were known initially as 'sunshine' camps. The impressive weight gains achieved by the children were a testament to Dr Gunn's methods. Summer camps were held in other locations, financed by donations and—from 1929—by the sale of what were originally known as Christmas seals, designed to raise funds voluntarily for purposes for which ordinary government and hospital board funds were not available. The first permanent health camp opened in 1932 at Otaki, in Southern Manawatu, on land donated by businessman and philanthropist Byron Brown.

In November 1929 the Christmas seal scheme underwent a change. To comply with international postal conventions, the planned supplementary 1d stamp was replaced by a 2d design that combined both duties—1d for postage and 1d for charity. At the same time the Minister of Health reported that a grateful ex-patient of a sanatorium at Pukeora, Hawke's Bay, had written in enthusiastic support of the campaign. Restored to full health, he had even sent £25 for 3000 of the new stamps.

But there was another significant change before New Zealand's first Health stamp went on sale on 11 December 1929. The artist was Leonard

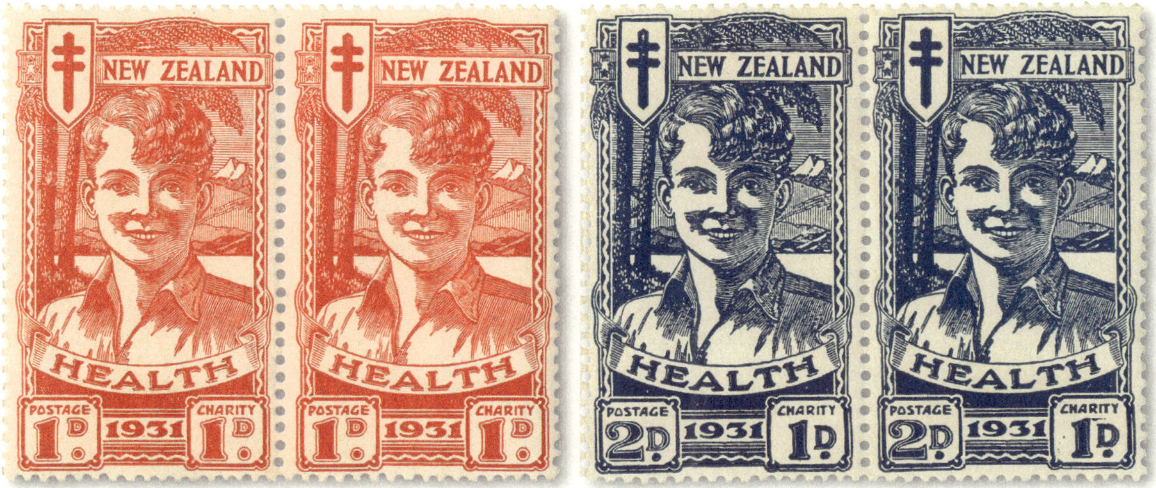

A smiling boy radiating well-being was the subject of the 1931 Health stamp designed by Leonard C. Mitchell. This became the most famous of all the Health issues and, unsurprisingly, the two stamps were known as the Red Boy and Blue Boy.

C. Mitchell (1901–72), who had trained at Palmerston North Technical School, but his intended design was replaced by his head-and-shoulders portrait of a registered nurse in uniform. She was surrounded on three sides by a border of Maori motifs, provided by the Government Printing Office, and supported by the slogan 'Help Stamp Out Tuberculosis.' The same basic design was also used for the following year's issue, the only major change being the new slogan 'Help Promote Health.'

The Health stamp design originally intended for 1930 (and perhaps 1929) finally appeared in 1931 but coincided with a worsening economic situation. Compared to previous years, sales were well down and as a result the Red

Original artwork for the 1932 Health stamp designed by William J.Cooch and R.E. Tripe of Wellington. The image of Hygeia is shown in wash (left) and converted to line (right) in preparation for plate-making.

In the final stamp (opposite) the Greek goddess of health and cleanliness poses on a pedestal and raises her glass (of medicinal wine) to the morning sun.

Boy and Blue Boy enjoyed rarity value and became the best-known of all New Zealand's Health stamps. They too were by Leonard C. Mitchell, and his smiling subjects radiated a sense of good health. The design incorporated the double-cross symbol of the International Anti-Tuberculosis Societies and a glimpse of New Zealand scenery similar to that in the country's first Airmail stamps, which were also by Mitchell and issued less than a fortnight later.

The next three Health stamps moved away from childhood themes, the 1932 issue in particular. It was designed by the Wellingtonians William J. Cooch and R.E. Tripe, and presented a scantily clad Hygeia, the ancient Greek goddess of health and cleanliness, posing on a pedestal with a snake and raising a glass to the rising sun. The snake, symbolising health, was frequently depicted drinking medicinal wine from Hygeia's cup, but she now had the appearance of a young woman greeting the dawn after an all-night party.

The 1932 Health stamp may have been intended as a tonic during the Depression. As for the designers' inspiration, it appears to owe much to an 1899 painting *Suspiria* ('Sigh'), by British neoclassicist artist Dorothy Tennant. Although both the title and presence of a cupid suggest Tennant's painting had an entirely different intent, the basic pose and state of (un) dress of the central female figure were very similar to that of New Zealand's

Hygeia. Perhaps one of the designers was related to Wellington artist Margaret E. Tripe, who specialised in nudes and portraits, and visited Europe regularly. She may have returned with a reproduction of *Suspiria*.

The rising sun motif reappeared—without Hygeia—on the 1933 Pathway to Health stamp, which was the first of many to be designed by James Berry. He submitted four schemes and was successful with a portrayal of a typically New Zealand scene, a path beside a cabbage tree leading through sandhills to a beach. But his design suffered during the etching process and took on a rather different sense. It was not entirely clear whether it depicted sunrise or sunset. In fact, Berry's own family referred to the stamp as 'The Pathway to Hell.'

A design by James Berry was also selected for the next Health issue, which benefited from production in England. The stamp suggested the campaign for children's health was going on the offensive, with its knight on a horse, a banner emblazoned 'health', and the message 'Crusade for Health 1934.' Sales for this stamp showed a slight improvement over previous years, but the outlook for Health issues was still far from positive, and camps derived more funds from general donations than the postal surcharge. However, following an intensive promotion in 1935, along with the introduction of first day covers and a generally improving economy, sales picked up and Health stamps became firmly established.

As if to reflect the improved outlook, the 1935 Health stamp—designed by S. Hall and the Post and Telegraph Department, Wellington—adopted a much sunnier disposition. The beach scene viewed through a keyhole marked a return to childhood themes, which would be maintained for the next two decades, while the reassuring rising sun motif made a further reappearance.

Hygeia, the subject of the 1932 stamp, will also be remembered as the source of such health-minded words as 'hygiene'. In 1937 Dr Elizabeth Gunn was appointed director of the New Zealand Health Department's Division of School Hygiene. After retiring she was awarded an MBE in 1951 and died in Wellington in 1963. Six years later she too became the subject of a Health stamp, and so helped raise funds for the movement she had founded half a century earlier.

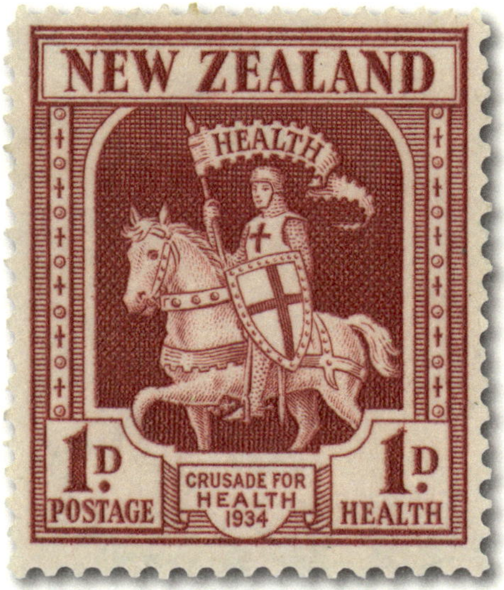

An armoured knight on horseback represented the crusade for child health in this 1934 issue. It was designed by James Berry, also responsible for the previous year's Pathway to Health.

Opposite: The Pathway to Health led past a cabbage tree towards the rising sun. James Berry's design for the 1933 Health stamp was in sharp contrast to Hygeia of the previous year.

9 off the ground

early airmail

In the late 19th century a succession of intrepid balloonists made ascents around New Zealand. The first was by a visiting American, the self-styled Professor Baldwin, who went aloft in an oiled silk and coal-gas-filled balloon above Dunedin's Caledonian Grounds on 21 January 1889. Before long, mail was also able to leave the ground, although not initially as a result of either this new technology or an initiative of the New Zealand Post and Telegraph Department.

This country's first 'airmail' service began in May 1897 on Great Barrier Island, whose sole link with Auckland was a weekly steamer service. Isolation prompted the establishment of a pigeon messenger service and what are claimed to be the world's first Airmail stamps, including the distinctive 1899 triangular issue showing a homing pigeon in full flight. It was designed by Irish-born draughtsman Harry Wrigg, who served in this country's land wars in the 1860s. He was awarded the New Zealand Cross for displaying

New Zealand's first official Airmail stamps took to the air in late 1931. Leonard C. Mitchell's design showed an early monoplane, with non-retractable wheels, passing between a heavy border and spectacular mountain scenery.

3D.
NEW ZEALAND
3D.
AIR MAIL

valour during another mail-related duty, the carrying of despatches through Maori territory.

Pigeon postage from Great Barrier Island was 6d, but the cost from Auckland was 1/-. According to the *Thames Star*, the increase reflected the difficulty of training birds to leave the city. They took an average of 55 minutes to fly the journey, and each could carry four messages, which were written or typed on tissue paper and attached around the birds' legs. The stamps were described as 'purely local in character' and 'were in no way to be confused with the ordinary postage stamps.' The secretary of the national Philatelic Society considered the whole initiative 'quite unnecessary' and warned stamp collectors against purchasing these 'labels [with] no philatelic status whatever.' The service was superseded in 1908 when an underwater telegraph cable was laid between the island and the mainland. By then the pigeon post stamps had been in service for some 11 years, considerably longer than the period covered by this country's official Airmail stamps, which did not appear for another 23 years.

There are claims for Temuka farmer and inventor Richard Pearse, but the first controlled and powered flight of a heavier-than-air craft in this country took place at Papakura, south of Auckland, on 5 February 1911. It was made by engineer Vivian Wright in a biplane he and his brother Leo had assembled from an imported kitset. Seven months later the world's first scheduled airmail service began in England, as part of the celebrations for the coronation of King George V, and public overseas airmail service began in 1919, between London and Paris. New Zealand was quick to recognise the advantages of the new system, and its first official airmail was carried in 1920, between Auckland and Dargaville. However regular services were another 16 years off.

In September 1928 Charles Kingsford Smith and C.T.P. Ulm made the first aerial crossing of the Tasman, from Sydney to Christchurch. The following year Imperial Airways introduced a service from Croydon, England, to Delhi, India. Flights were gradually extended eastwards to Calcutta and Singapore until they reached Darwin, Australia, where they connected with Qantas services. As a result, by 1934 mail could be flown from London to Sydney but, until the introduction of a trans-Tasman airmail service in 1940, needed to be shipped across to New Zealand.

New Zealand's first Airmail stamps were issued in November 1931. Although four years before the country's first regular services, the stamps could be used for mail which would connect with airmail services overseas. The stamps carried on the typical New Zealand lake and bush scene as pioneered by the 1898 Pictorials, but there was now an aeroplane overhead, negotiating a heavy border. The design, by Leonard C. Mitchell, was criticised, but the growing demand for airmail services gave the Post Office

Opposite: Arguably the world's first airmail stamps were those required for the Pigeongram service, between Great Barrier Island and Auckland, which began in 1897. The triangular stamps were in use from 1899. The service continued until 1908, 23 years before New Zealand issued its first official Airmail stamp.

a timely opportunity to release a new set of stamps. A competition was announced, with £25 to be paid for each accepted design. The 75 competitors included James Berry, responsible for the Health issues of 1933 and 1934. His initial designs for the second Airmail issue were not accepted but he was undaunted, and submitted further unsolicited ideas. It was the arrival at Bell Block aerodrome, New Plymouth on 12 April 1934 of Ulm in the 'Faith in Australia', bringing the first official airmail from that country, that inspired a new and ultimately successful approach. Berry based his design on a photograph taken by New Plymouth chemist Arthur H. Blennerhassett. He included a prominent tree fern and a cloaked Maori, balanced by the hangar and activities of a 'New Zealand air terminal', all set against a backdrop of snowclad Mt Taranaki/ Egmont. Berry's design did not in fact depict Ulm's 'Faith in Australia', an Avro X monoplane, but a De Havilland Rapide biplane.

The 7d and highest denomination in New Zealand's first Airmail stamps of 1931, designed by Leonard C. Mitchell.

Compared to Mitchell's 1931 design, Berry's mail-carrying aeroplane now had the benefit of open skies, constrained only by a simple border. The emphasis was on the aircraft itself, easily spotted against a bank of white cloud and positioned between the centrally placed lettering and denominations. This reflected

Berry's stated philosophy: 'The main portion of the design should be clear and easily distinguished in stamp size. The lettering should tie in with the design and be well balanced for size and weight.'

The second Airmail stamps were issued in May 1935 and in three values: 1d, 3d and 6d. They arrived some four months after this country's first regular airmail services, which had begun between Hokitika and Okuru in Westland, and were soon extended to the main centres. The combination of three local enterprises—East Coast Airlines, Union Airways and Cook Strait Airways (which all became part of NAC, National Airways Corporation in 1945)—resulted in a growing network. Postage on mail carried by this fleet was 2d, resulting in a high demand for the red 1d stamps, but there was less call on the 3d and 6d values. The 1d stamp remained in service until late 1938 and was the last special Airmail stamp to be issued by New Zealand. Since then, ordinary stamps have done the job, along with stickers and labels to indicate which mail is required to take to the air.

Rising costs during the Depression demanded an additional Airmail stamp in 1931, and so the 3d value (originally brown) was reprinted in green and overprinted 'Five Pence'.

6D NEW ZEALAND 6D
AIR MAIL

Opposite: Preliminary pencil drawing by James Berry for the second issue of Airmail stamps, in 1935. A biplane comes in to land at New Plymouth's Bell Block aerodrome, observed by a pair of Maori standing beneath a tree fern on the left. A snowclad Mt Taranaki/ Egmont is seen in the distance.

The 1935 Airmail stamps appeared in three denominations: 1d, 3d and 6d. All depicted a 'New Zealand air terminal', obviously Bell Block in view of Mt Taranaki/Egmont in the background. One of the standing Maori in Berry's original drawing is now sitting beneath the tree fern.

10 fiscal duties

the 1931 arms type

The 2/6 Arms Type fiscal stamp of 1931, designed by H. Linley Richardson. As the name suggests, elements of the New Zealand coat of arms have been modified to fit the format and framed on either side by decorative borders composed of Maori patterns.

In 1866 the first submarine telegraph cable was laid across Cook Strait, improving communications around New Zealand. In that same year the colony's letter writers were also introduced to a new application for postage stamps. Under the new Stamp Duties Act they could now be used for fiscal purposes, such as the payment of duties on 'deeds and other instruments relating to transactions between living persons.' In the case of an inheritance, for example, when the successor was directly related to the predecessor, the duty was one percent of the value of the property. But at the other end of the scale, when the successor was 'a stranger in blood' to the other, the duty was a much stiffer 10 percent. The new legislation—generally known as the Stamp Act—required the issue of special stamps. These were for revenue-gathering, such as the payment of fees and fines, but were not available for normal postage duties. However, in 1882 the Second Sidefaces (pp. 19–23), issued in denominations from ½d to 1d, were intended for both purposes

TWO SHILLINGS
ONWARD
NEW ZEALAND STAMP DUTY
AND SIXPENCE

New Zealand's first Postal Fiscal stamps, which could also be used for both duty paying and postage purposes, were issued in 1882. Queen Victoria was shown in sideface, in values from 1d to £1.

and were therefore inscribed 'postage and revenue'. At the same time there was an issue of the first Postal Fiscals. As the name suggests, they were primarily for revenue purposes, but some could also be used for postage. Rectangular and larger than the Sidefaces, they also depicted a left-facing Queen Victoria and came in 21 denominations ranging from 1d to £1.

In 1900 the *Otago Witness* claimed New Zealand made more use of these fiscal stamps than any other stamp-issuing country. In their non-postage role these stamps were most likely to be attached to legal documents and were also used on telegrams. As such they were the subject of the so-called 'Stamp Case' in 1895, when two men were acquitted, in the Wellington Supreme Court, on a charge of removing cancelled fiscal stamps off telegrams stolen from the Telegraph Department's store.

In 1915, after the first Postal Fiscals had been in use for some 33 years, H. Linley Richardson was approached to design a new set. It proved an extremely drawn-out process, for the replacements, known as the Arms Type, did not finally appear until 1931. Richardson's preliminary design featured the Royal Arms of the United Kingdom, which includes several images of lions, both 'passant' and 'statant' and with one wearing the imperial crown. When this approach was not considered suitable he offered one with more local relevance and which owed much to a suggestion he had provided for a George V stamp in 1911. It depicted the king in an oval with the background figures of Zealandia and a Maori warrior, inspired by the two supporters on the recently granted New Zealand coat of arms. For his new fiscal design Richardson simplified and compressed the main elements of the arms—the supporters, flag-bearing lion crest, shield and 'Onward' motto—into a rectangular format. In particular, modification was needed to accommodate Zealandia's flag and the warrior's taiaha. Also, while the two supporters in the original arms had avoided one another (although they turned to acknowledge one another in a 1956 update), Richardson presented them as if in transition, gazing directly ahead. His scheme also retained a lion—strictly speaking a 'demi-Lion rampant guardant Or'—flying the British Union Jack.

The design project now stalled, presumably because of restrictions resulting from the First World War. It was reactivated in 1924, and Richardson's scheme underwent further modification to fit a near-square format, as adopted by new 2/- and 3/- George V stamps, which he was now also designing. In addition, the Union Jack was replaced with the New Zealand flag, and because of the need for extra width in relation to height, Richardson was able to make good use of the diamond motifs and Maori rafter patterns which he had introduced on earlier designs, and these were now placed down each side of the stamp.

There were even more changes when Richardson was asked to provide

five variations in the borders at the sides of the stamps. This was so that the planned 46 different denominations, from 1/3d to £1000, could be grouped and distinguished more easily. These variants included vertical, curved and diagonal arrangements, all containing the same—or similar—elements he had used in the 1915 and the (now released) 1926 George V issues. But with this attended to, there was yet another hold-up before the stamps appeared. Two likely causes for this were the controversy over the 1926 Admiral and Field Marshall designs, and concern over production standards. Finally, the Royal Mint's tender for the production of the dies was accepted, and printing was then carried out by the Government Printing Office in New Zealand.

The design stages had dragged on for some 16 years, and the first of the Arms Type stamps were issued in 1931, by which time Richardson was 51 years old. He died in 1947, but his stamps lived on. By 1960, when more modern methods enabled the payment of duty without the need for stamps, most of the high values had been withdrawn from sale. The seven remaining were reduced to four in 1967, when the stamps were replaced by their decimal equivalents. Since then, further improvements to technology and the arrival of computers have replaced the need for paper stamps to collect duty, while duty itself has been abolished in such areas as shares, mortgages and residential property. The remainder of the Arms Type stamps were finally withdrawn in the late 1980s, after nearly six decades of duty.

H. Linley Richardson managed the unique achievement of combining a career in fine arts with that of stamp designing. As previously noted, James Nairn and Louis J. Steele were highly regarded New Zealand painters, but they were responsible for two extremely unsatisfactory stamp designs, for the 1900 South African (Boer) War (pp. 30–31) and the 1906 Christchurch Exhibition (pp. 43, 45–47) respectively. The small scale associated with stamp design demanded that it become a specialist area, and one which was dominated in this country, from the 1940s through to the 1960s, by Leonard C. Mitchell and James Berry. But while fine artists were not generally responsible for designing our postage stamps, they did provide essential images. The first of a series of stamps reproducing paintings by well-known painters appeared in 1973, honoring Frances Hodgkins, and was followed by others illustrating the achievements of Rita Angus (1983), Colin McCahon (1997) and Peter McIntyre (1998).

When an increase in postal rates in 1950 created an unprecedented demand for 1½d stamps, the blank Arms Type design was overprinted '1½d Postage'. Unlike other Arms Type stamps, this was used solely for postage purposes.

Opposite: Three of the border designs H. Linley Richardson provided for the 1931 Arms Type duty stamps. These variations were intended to assist the differentiation between the large number of values in this issue.

11 a natural history

tuatara to Mt Cook

The lowest value in New Zealand's second set of Pictorial stamps, issued in 1935, was the Fantail, or piwakawaka. Designer J. Fitzgerald placed the sociable native bird among clematis, usually found near the edge of the forest.

Having already celebrated several native birds on stamps, in 1935 New Zealand gave postal prominence to one of the most unusual and ancient of all its creatures. The tuatara, a lizard-like reptile, had long been known to the Maori, who regarded it as the messenger of Whiro, the god of death and darkness. It had come to the attention of Europeans in the 1830s, and was sketched by missionary and naturalist Richard Taylor. He reproduced it for the first time in his 1855 book *Te Ika a Maui,* and two years later a specimen taken to England was the basis for an illustration in another book, by the keeper of zoology at the British Museum. Science later realised this curious creature dated from a time when giant reptiles ruled the earth. The dinosaurs, iguanodons and ichthyosaurus had all become extinct, but New Zealand's tuatara was a survivor.

For its postal debut the tuatara was drawn by Leonard C. Mitchell. His exquisitely detailed reptile was typically immobile, poised as if in a state of

POSTAGE
AND
REVENUE
1/2 D
NEW ZEALAND

NEW ZEALAND
TUATARA
8D.
POSTAGE
& REVENUE
8D.

NEW ZEALAND
TUATARA
8D.
POSTAGE
& REVENUE
8D.

The 8d Tuatara, designed by Leonard C. Mitchell. Shown are the original artwork in continuous tone (wash), a drawing in which tones have been converted to line and the stamp as printed.

The tui is distinguished by its melodious song, iridescent wing and neck feathers, and tufts of white feathers at its throat. Line drawing from design by M. King.

Opposite: The 1/- Tui, which joined the Fantail (½d) and Kiwi (1d) in the 1935 Pictorials. Thirty-seven years earlier, the Huia (3d), Kiwi (6d), and Kea and Kaka (1/-) had been included in the First Pictorials.

high alert, on a strategic rock. In an article also published in 1935, Auckland War Memorial Museum ornithologist Robert Falla described the tuatara as 'unwilling to move unless hard-pressed.' But while it was inclined to remain still for long periods, as when enjoying the warmth of the sun, it could also move quickly if the need arose. This conservation of energy may explain why the tuatara can apparently live to a considerable age. Falla felt it had the right attitude towards life, writing: 'In an age of bustle it is refreshing even to think of the existence of creatures that belong to an age when time did not matter, and whose rule for long life seems to be—don't eat more than necessary, rest when possible, and don't worry.'

The year 1935 was important for the tuatara. As well as being selected for a postage stamp, it was the subject of an article in the American *National Geographic Magazine*. The writer, geneticist Frieda Cobb Blanchard, PhD, had learned about the tuatara at university in the United States and came to New Zealand to study her subjects at first hand. The story of her visit to Stephens Island, the tuatara sanctuary in Marlborough Sounds, appeared under the following lengthy title: 'Tuatara: "Living Fossils" Walk on Well-Nigh

Inaccessible Rocky Islands off the Coast of New Zealand.'

In life the tuatara has a greenish brown and wrinkled leather-like skin. The impressive spiny crest running down the middle of its back had inspired its name, tuatara meaning 'peaks on the back' in Maori. The spines are the remains of a defence mechanism developed by the reptile's ancient ancestors, while its teeth represent another link with the age of dinosaurs. Because they are sharp projections of the jawbone and not detachable, as in most animals, Falla suggested the tuatara would be unable to distinguish between toothache and headache.

The 2½d Mt Cook by Leonard C. Mitchell, in the 1935 Pictorials. New Zealand's highest peak was framed by side panels of Mt Cook buttercup. It had previously been the subject of two stamps (½d and 5/-) in the 1898 Pictorials.

The tuatara was classified as an endangered species in 1895. Forty years later, and along with 13 other designs, it was selected for New Zealand's second set of Pictorial stamps. They were released during a period of great social change, following the election of the country's first Labour Government.

The new stamps also appeared at a time when local painters were developing a more distinctly New Zealand way of looking at things. This resulted in such well-known images as Christopher Perkins' *Taranaki* (1932), a view of a dairy factory and the mountain then generally known as Egmont, and Rita Angus's *Cass* (c. 1936-37), of an inland Canterbury railway station. New Zealanders were also becoming familiar with local images circulating on their first official banknotes, following the incorporation of the Reserve Bank in 1934. These replaced notes issued previously by trading banks, and carried images of the kiwi, Mitre Peak and Tawhaio, the second Maori King.

Like the original 1898 Pictorials, the new stamps were distinguished by a diversity of designs and formats. Natural scenery and native birds remained dominant themes. Aoraki/Mt Cook and Mitre Peak both re-appeared, and Mt Taranaki/Egmont was selected for the highest denomination. The set also included Captain Cook coming ashore at Poverty Bay on 8 October 1769, and a striped marlin, which promoted New Zealand as a big-game paradise. A horse-drawn crop harvester represented the importance of agriculture, suggesting the country was not yet ready to acknowledge its huge debt to sheep on postage stamps. A major innovation was the use of Maori subjects and design elements, such as the circular carving pattern and spiral motifs framing the tuatara.

Leonard C. Mitchell's huge contribution to local postal imagery had begun with the first Health stamp in 1929, and he had four designs accepted for 1935 Pictorials—far more than any other artist. His stamps were distinguished by their quality and clarity and, in addition to the Tuatara (8d) included

The 3/- Taranaki /Mt Egmont was one of four designs by Leonard C. Mitchell accepted for the 1935 Pictorials, and continued the theme of mountain and alpine views established in the 1898 Pictorials.

POSTAGE & REVENUE
SWORDFISH
5D
5D
NEW ZEALAND

Mt Cook (2½d), the Wahine (or 'Maori Girl') (3d), and Mt Taranaki/Egmont (3/-). His Mt Cook and Mt Taranaki/Egmont were larger format stamps, of scenic panoramas framed by decorative borders. Thus New Zealand's highest peak was seen beyond clusters of one of the most distinctive members of its alpine flora, the Mt Cook buttercup (erroneously known as the Mt Cook Lily), *Ranunculus lyalli*, the largest buttercup in the world and found only on the mountains of the South Island.

New Zealand had waited nearly four decades for this second full set of Pictorial stamps, but only 25 years elapsed before it received another. The third issue, in 1960, heralded some dramatic developments; the number of stamps ballooned to 23, and the heavy borders which had circumscribed designs of the past had now disappeared. The subjects' backgrounds were now mostly plain and unadorned, and extended to the edges of the stamp. But one thing that didn't change was the input of Leonard C. Mitchell; he was responsible for two of the new designs (the butter industry and the Sutherland Falls), while his son Allan provided another seven.

In 1991, 56 years after its postal debut, the tuatara was given its own set of stamps. Designed by Pauline Morse of Pukerua Bay and released in conjunction with the World Wide Fund for Nature, depicted the tuatara in its preferred activity, outdoors sunbathing, while one specimen opted for the privacy of its burrow.

The 5d Swordfish, designed by William J. Cooch and R.E. Tripe (also responsible for Hygeia, the 1932 Health stamp), represented the sport of big-game fishing in the 1935 Pictorials. The striped marlin leaps from the water in front of the 'hole in the rock' on Piercy Island, Bay of Islands. Side panels of Maori woodcarving patterns are surmounted by the prows of war canoes.

12 features of the dominion

Maori motifs

The world of the Maori was on the mind of a number of artists who offered designs for New Zealand's first set of Pictorial postage stamps, to be issued in 1898. The noms-de-plume used by some of the more successful entrants included 'Arawa', 'Aotearoa', 'Mahi', 'Tongariro' and 'Maori'. But there was no Maori content as such in the stamps themselves, apart from the placenames Ruapehu, Otira and Wakatipu, the latter being also misspelled Wakitipu (p. 28). Eight years later, the arrival of the Te Arawa canoe and the art of Maori woodcarving were included in the 1906 Christchurch Exhibition stamps (pp. 48–49), but these suffered from poor-quality printing and overwhelming frames so were neither impressive nor enthusiastic celebrations of Maori culture.

A Maori woman lowering a kete (basket) of food into a boiling spring for cooking. This design, by M. Mathews, included side panels inspired by Maori woodcarving.

It was inevitable that elements of Maori carving design would be used to add a distinctive local flavour to this country's stamps. The first such move was when H. Linley Richardson combined an adaptation of a Maori rafter pattern

POSTAGE & REVENUE
D 1½
D 1½
NEW ZEALAND

NEW ZEALAND
POSTAGE
REVENUE
3
THREE PENCE
3

with a crown and the Southern Cross to form an elegant border around his George V stamp of 1915 (pp. 62 & 63). Richardson continued this use of Maori borders, introducing them into his 1925 Dunedin Exhibition stamps and the George V Admirals of the following year (pp. 58 & 59). In the meantime, New Zealand's 1920 Victory set, which was designed in England, had included the portrait of a Maori male with moko (facial tattoo) (pp. 70 & 71). In view of the set's liberal use of British lions and female figures to represent peace and victory, this Maori was equally symbolic and not a true reflection of the individuals who had participated in the recent war.

In 1931 the New Zealand Post and Telegraph Department announced a competition for a second set of Pictorial stamps. It was open to artists from all over the world and prizes of £25 were offered for each design accepted. The stated aim of the stamps was to offer 'a representation of characteristic or notable New Zealand scenery or genre, or industrial, agricultural, or pastoral scene,' all in the interests of promoting this country abroad, especially to Great Britain. Although still heavily dependent on the Mother Country, New Zealand now wished to be seen as a more independent-minded nation. There was a large number of unsuccessful entries featuring Maori subjects, with variations on the whare, canoe, tiki and The Rangitira (chief), while one overlapped outlines of New Zealand and Britain to reinforce the message that this was the 'Britain of the South.' Agriculture, including poultry farming, was also well represented, with

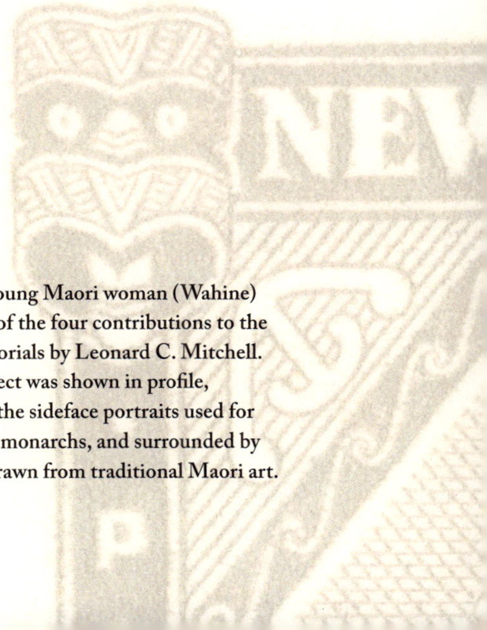

The 3d young Maori woman (Wahine) was one of the four contributions to the 1935 Pictorials by Leonard C. Mitchell. The subject was shown in profile, echoing the sideface portraits used for reigning monarchs, and surrounded by motifs drawn from traditional Maori art.

another (also unsuccessful) design combining Maori ornament and the message 'The finest wool and mutton in the world.'

Over 1500 submissions were received, and from these a special adjudication board selected 14 designs according to several categories: New Zealand plant and animal life, scenery, Maori subjects, agricultural and pastoral, history, sport and Maori art. The new set went on sale on 1 May 1935, whereupon the *New Zealand Herald* announced that 'the issue of Georgian stamps to which New Zealanders have become accustomed during the last 20 years' had been withdrawn from circulation. Further, their replacements, presenting 'characteristic features of the Dominion,' were nothing less than 'a complete transformation' in the country's postage stamps.

That the new set had overseas tourism in mind was shown by the choice of a striped marlin and big-game fishing to represent sport (p. 102). Three of the four Maori designs had similar aspirations, showing exotic and historical aspects: cooking of food in a natural boiling spring, a young Maori woman (wahine) wearing a woven headband, huia feather and greenstone tiki, and a traditional pre-European house, or whare. Historical continuity was provided by the designer of the third of those stamps, H.W. Young, who was also responsible for the Mt Cook stamp in the original Pictorial set, 37 years earlier. The fourth Maori design, and perhaps the most innovative in the whole 1935 set, was by I.F. Calder and based on the Maori ornamentation used on sliding door panels, or tatau. Apart from early fiscal stamps whose designs were dominated by numerals, this red and black design (later printings were in red and grey) was the first purely decorative scheme to be used on a New Zealand stamp.

Not surprisingly, there were borders of Maori motifs on other stamps in the set, including a tribute to agriculture. That design, of a harvesting scene, was the only one not by a New Zealander. It was provided by Mr. T.I. Archer, an engraver attached to the Indian Government Printing Office. The release of the 1935 Pictorials also heralded a particularly busy period for the stamps of New Zealand. Within a week the country was presented with two further new sets, one commemorating King George V's silver jubilee, and the other issued in connection with Sir Charles Kingsford Smith's forthcoming trans-Tasman Silver Jubilee flight.

For its Centennial stamp issue in 1940 New Zealand reflected on its historic links with Britain, and the now-expected Maori themes adopted a similar view. But two decades later, the issue of a Third Pictorial set gave

Maori hei tiki, the greenstone neck pendant, as designed by James Berry for the 1960 Pictorials. Compared to previous Pictorial issues, this tiki was seen without any enclosing or decorative border. This stamp was included in the decimalised Pictorials of 1967 and, as a 15c stamp, later reappeared in different colours.

Opposite: H.W. Young's Maori meeting house (whare) for the 1935 Pictorials, flanked by two other distinctive features of New Zealand, the tree fern (left) and cabbage tree (right).

POSTAGE & REVENUE
9D. NEW ZEALAND 9D.

POSTAGE & REVENUE
9D. NEW ZEALAND 9D.

Original line drawing and colour artwork (opposite) by I.F. Calder, for the 9d stamp (left) in the 1935 Pictorials. Based on ornamentation on a Maori door panel, this was the first purely decorative design to be used on a non-fiscal New Zealand stamp.

The 15c Maori fish hook (designed by Mark Cleverley), and 20c tattoo (moko) pattern (designed by Enid Hunter) in the 1970–71 Definitives. The 11c maripi, carved wooden knife, and 13c wahaika, handclub, were designed by Allan Mitchell for a 1976 issue featuring maori artefacts collected during Captain Cook's voyages.

Opposite: Patu, carved wooden club for close combat fighting and ceremonial purposes. This 18c stamp in the 1970–71 Definitives was designed by Enid Hunter.

the country another chance to determine how it wished to be presented to the world. The 10 lowest values were now given over to native flowers, while there were also the usual references to local industry, tourism and Maori subjects, but the big difference between this and previous Pictorials was that it broke free of the decorative border. As a result, the two Maori subjects—a greenstone hei tiki (designed by James Berry) and a representation of early South Island rock art (designed by D.F. Kee)—were seen against plain backgrounds. A decade later saw a further development, when the three Maori subjects in the 1970–71 Definitives received a much more simplified and graphic treatment.

Maori art had experienced a tentative introduction to New Zealand stamps in the early 1900s and initially was largely marginalised and reserved for decorative purposes. Although represented in the first three Pictorial sets, it was not until the late 1980s that it became the subject of separate issues, such as fibre arts (1987) and rafter paintings (1989). Then, in 1990, when New Zealand marked the 150th anniversary of the Treaty of Waitangi, a set of six stamps (designed by K. Hall of Christchurch) recognised the heritage of the Maori people. This was followed by others celebrating specific aspects of the culture of the country's original settlers (the tangata whenua), including myths (1994), language (1995) and craft (1996).

13 on a hostile shore

ANZAC

To date the only references by New Zealand stamps to the country's military exploits overseas had been the South African war design of 1900 (pp. 30 & 31), a George V overprinted 'War Stamp' in 1915 and, indirectly, the 1920 Victory issue (pp. 64–71). Then in 1936 two New Zealand stamps marked the 21st anniversary of the country's best-known military campaign, at Gallipoli in Turkey. In the tradition now well established by Health issues, those stamps also served as fundraisers. The ½d (green) and 1d (red) postage values sold for double those amounts, the extra going to the assistance of members of the Returned Soldiers' Association.

New Zealanders may have seen their first references to Gallipoli in news reports from the war between Turkey and Russia in the 1870s. But the name took on a greater significance some four decades later, when Turkey's entry into the First World War in 1914 posed a threat. Britain's response was to secure the Dardanelles, the narrow strait in Turkey that

Marking the 50th anniversary of the landing at Gallipoli in 1965, R. Maurice Conly's 5d stamp shows Anzac Cove with its steep cliffs in the background. It includes a red poppy, which grew at Gallipoli, to recognise the later service by New Zealand soldiers in France and Belgium.

ANZAC
1915
1965
5D
NEW ZEALAND

Photograph of an unknown New Zealand soldier, used as a basis by Leonard C. Mitchell for the 1936 stamp commemorating the 21st anniversary of the Anzac landing at Gallipoli. The soldier is seen posing with his boot on a sack of cane sugar, replaced by a pile of sandbags in the artwork (right). The two 1936 stamps (opposite) were fundraisers, to assist members of the Returned Soldiers' Association.

NEW ZEALAND
1/2D POSTAGE
N·Z·R·S·A 1/2D
1915 ANZAC 1936
TWENTY FIRST ANNIVERSARY

NEW ZEALAND
1D POSTAGE
N·Z·R·S·A 1D
1915 ANZAC 1936
TWENTY FIRST ANNIVERSARY

Unlike the 5d stamp, the 4d Anzac commemorative of 1965 did not include the red poppy. R. Maurice Conly's design shows the barren cliffs of Gallipoli which confronted the New Zealand troops in 1915.

was part of a vital sea link between the Mediterranean and the Black Sea. An attempt to force the Dardanelles with naval power failed and so ground troops—Australians and New Zealanders, alongside British and French units—were sent in.

Troops began going ashore on the Gallipoli Peninsula at dawn on 25 April 1915. The first reports New Zealand received were that the landing was 'completely successful', despite serious opposition by the enemy 'behind strong entrenchments and entanglements.' A few days later the governor informed Prime Minister William Massey that he had received a telegram from the king, offering congratulations on the 'splendid conduct and bravery displayed by the New Zealand troops at the Dardanelles, who have proved themselves worthy sons of the Empire.'

But there were terrible casualties, and reports were slow to emerge. An item in the *Evening Post* of 4 May explained that the difficulties of the Gallipoli campaign were 'enormously greater' than those experienced by the troops in France. The New Zealanders had been landed on 'a hostile shore' and had begun at once to fight their way forward, leaving lines of communication behind them.

The Australian and New Zealand forces—soon to be known as ANZACs—held a tenuous grip for nearly eight months. But withdrawal was the only option and was carried out successfully in mid-December.

Altogether 11,600 New Zealanders served on Gallipoli, and suffered an appallingly high casualty rate of 2721 dead and 4752 wounded. The first memorial service was held in 1916 on 25 April, which became known as Anzac Day, and in 1920 was declared a public holiday. In the following year the New Zealand Returned Soldiers' Association adopted as an emblem the red poppy of Flanders. Anzac Day later came to be observed as a commemoration of all New Zealanders who had died in the First World War and in 1949 was extended to include those of the South African and Second World wars.

Financial constraints in the 1930s resulted in reductions in the size of the New Zealand Army, but as the decade progressed the growing concerns for developments in Europe and Asia stimulated a recruitment campaign. On 27 April 1936, shortly after Hitler sent troops into the demilitarised Rhineland, New Zealand remembered the sacrifice at Gallipoli with its first strictly anniversary stamps. In the continuing spirit of Anzac they were printed in Australia and showed a New Zealand soldier shouldering a bayoneted rifle and wearing the distinctive 'lemon-squeezer' hat which was adopted during the First World War. He stood with his foot on a sandbag, against a background of Anzac Cove. Leonard C. Mitchell based his design on a recent photograph of a soldier posing in uniform but with a sack of cane sugar.

Twenty-nine years later, and following a suggestion by the Returned Services' Association, the New Zealand Post Office recognised the 50th anniversary of the landing at Gallipoli. Plans to produce a joint issue with Australia came to nothing, and so this country went ahead with a design by Christchurch artist R. Maurice Conly. He was one of 10 designers who submitted roughs for the issue and was successful with his elevated view looking down on Anzac Cove, showing the steep cliffs that had confronted the New Zealanders coming ashore in 1915. His design also incorporated a poppy, which was the cause of some debate. There were suggestions that it related to action in Flanders rather than Gallipoli, but as Conly explains in his story, *Send For The Artist*, those flowers 'grew in profusion at Gallipoli and a charge was made by the New Zealanders across a field of red poppies.' An area south of the beach where the Anzac troops landed was named Poppy Valley for obvious reasons, while a visitor to the valley in 1919 reported there were now apricot trees and date palms, a result of stones left by Australian troops. Conly's 1965 design was issued in two variations: the 5d with a poppy, as originally intended, and the 4d without.

Despite the passage of time, attendances at the nation's annual Anzac Day remembrance services during the 21st century continue to remain strong. Reflecting this, New Zealand Post began a series of issues to mark the Anzac spirit forged at Gallipoli, and the first in 2008 acknowledged the costly failure at the Dardanelles. The third set, in 2010, included the silhouette of a present-day New Zealand soldier, wearing a 'lemon squeezer'. And in the spirit of Leonard C. Mitchell, who used a photograph for his 1936 stamp, its modern equivalent (by Cue Design, Wellington) was based on a photograph taken by journalism student Shane Cowlishaw. It showed a soldier at The Tomb of the Unknown Soldier, Wellington, at dawn on Anzac Day 2008.

Wearing the traditional 'lemon squeezer' hat, a New Zealand serviceman soldier stands guard at The Tomb of the Unknown Soldier in Wellington, during the dawn ceremony on Anzac Day, 25 April, 2008.

14 abdication and coronation

Edward VIII & George VI

The coronation of George VI took place at Westminster Abbey on 12 May 1937. Ten months later New Zealand began issuing a set of George VI stamps, with the highest value, 3/-, appearing in 1947. The stamps were designed by the printers in England, while William J. Cooch of Wellington was responsible for the frames in the lower (pence) values.

During the 1930s the British Empire experienced a succession of royal events, most of which naturally demanded the issue of postage stamps. But such was the pace of change that the New Zealand Post Office wasn't always able to keep up.

On 6 May 1935 King George V and Queen Mary celebrated the silver jubilee of their accession to the throne. Late the previous year James Berry had been invited to submit designs for a set of stamps to mark the occasion. It was his first attempt at portraiture, and he sought advice as to whether the queen's head should be placed to the left or right of the king's. In the end the English printers used photographs instead of Berry's portraits, although his border incorporating the Southern Cross was retained. George V was a heavy smoker and suffered from a number of illnesses, and died a little less than eight months after the silver

NEW ZEALAND
3/-
POSTAGE
& REVENUE
3/-

jubilee. Berry now offered a design for a commemorative stamp, combining a portrait of the king with a view of the House of Parliament, Wellington, but the idea did not proceed.

George V's eldest son, Edward, ascended the throne on 20 January 1936. Initially Britain decided to produce three separate and successive issues of stamps depicting the new king, two to mark the accession and coronation and then a permanent set. The first drawings submitted showed Edward VIII in the uniform of Colonel-in-Chief of the Seaforth Highlanders, a historic British Army regiment associated with northern Scotland. Edward had worn the uniform when representing the king at a levee at Buckingham Palace in March 1935, but this image was rejected in favour of a profile based on a photograph.

Britain's Edward VIII stamps were issued in September 1936. They differed from that country's previous stamps, which was said to reflect the king's desire for simplicity and change. But there was a major change just three months later when Edward faced government disapproval of his planned marriage to American divorcée Wallis Simpson. To avoid a constitutional crisis he gave

1935 stamp commemorating the silver jubilee of King George V and Queen Mary. The English printers based the royal portraits on photographs, while James Berry designed the border, which incorporated the Southern Cross.

up the throne after a reign of just 10 months and 22 days, the shortest since King Harold's rule of just over nine months ended in 1066. And because Edward had abdicated before the end of the customary one-year period between accession and coronation, he went uncrowned.

On 11 December 1936 New Zealand received a message from the king advising that he had 'executed an instrument of abdication.' The following day, as required by the Demise of the Crown Act of 1908, the governor-general reassured New Zealanders that nothing would be affected; in fact, it would be as if 'no such demise had happened.' He also advised that at 2.30 pm on 14 December a proclamation announcing that 'the Imperial Crown of Great Britain, Ireland and all other His former Majesty's Dominions is now solely and rightfully come to the High and Mighty Prince Albert Frederick Arthur George' would be read in front of Parliament Buildings, Wellington.

New Zealand had plans to issue Edward VIII postage stamps but, as in Australia, none eventuated. However, Edward would later be included, along with four other monarchs, on one of the 1940 Centennial stamps

The 1935 Silver Jubilee issue consisted of three values—½d, 1d (shown here) and 6d. The Southern Cross appears above Their Majesties, who are flanked by panels of traditional Maori patterns.

At the suggestion of James Berry, the 1940 Centennial issue included this stamp recording all the British sovereigns of New Zealand. Berry also intended the stamp to represent this country's loyalty to the British throne, and flanked the ruling monarch, George VI, with smaller sideface portraits of his predecessors. They included the only appearance to date on a New Zealand stamp of Edward VIII, who abdicated in 1936.

and also in a set of all (six) monarchs to date on the 150th anniversary of postage stamps, in 1990. Back in 1936 William J. Cooch, partly responsible for the Hygeia Health stamp in 1932, had provided drawings for an Edward VIII issue. These included the king in the uniform of the Seaforth Highlanders, and an amended design got as far as die proof stage. James Berry also offered several designs which were not accepted by the Post Office and they included two portraits in military uniform. When he was Prince of Wales, Edward had been keen to serve during the First World War. As heir to the throne he was not permitted to do so, but he did visit the front line when he could and for this was awarded the Military Cross in 1916.

Following the abdication, Edward VIII was succeeded by his younger brother, who became George VI. He and his wife Queen Elizabeth were crowned at Westminster Abbey on 12 May 1937, and as a result of recent events the coronation was a much anticipated and glittering occasion. In the words of the *New Zealand Herald*: 'This is a day of days for the British people. Citizens of an Empire on which the sun is ever rising, they greet its dawn with gladness as it comes with a summons to fill the following hours with a happy festival.' It also pointed out that New Zealand was, in fact, 'the first of the Dominions to be awakened thus.'

The royal occasion was marked in this country by a wide range of special events and pageants. There were coronation balls at Cambridge and Pakuranga, while the main feature at the Hawke's Bay Jockey Club meeting was the Coronation Cup. Bands played at locations around central Auckland and at 9.30 pm, when the king and queen entered Westminster Abbey, they all struck up the National Anthem. The Queen City also had the usual illuminations, which were said to be even more impressive the next day after rain produced reflections on the wet road surfaces.

The day following the celebrations, Coronation stamps went on sale in New Zealand. In anticipation, a queue had already formed at Auckland's Central Post Office by 8 am. Designed and printed in England, the stamps were very similar in format to those marking the silver jubilee of two years earlier. Portraits of the royal couple were surrounded by a decorative border, the main difference being in the local reference—the New Zealand coat of arms had replaced the Southern Cross.

With a new king on the throne, New Zealanders now turned to the prospect of a personal visit by Their Majesties. The *New Zealand*

The coronation of George VI and Queen Elizabeth in May 1937 was celebrated in New Zealand by an issue of three stamps. Their design echoed that of the Silver Jubilee stamp of 1935 and was carried out by the printers Bradbury Wilkinson in England.

Details of decorative borders, by an unknown designer, proposed but not accepted for the 1938 George VI issue.

Herald believed the enthusiasm for such an event would far exceed that for the recent coronation celebrations and suggested 1940, when New Zealand would be marking its centennial, as an appropriate time. The outbreak of war would have interrupted any such plans. While royal visits to New Zealand were planned for both 1949 and 1952, both were cancelled on account of the king's health. To mark the first of these, the indefatigable James Berry submitted a number of designs, three of which were accepted after much simplification and modification. On this occasion the set of four stamps was actually printed but destroyed when the tour was cancelled. Berry was then asked to provide amended designs for the 1952 tour but they did not proceed when that visit was also cancelled.

George VI didn't come to New Zealand but this country released a set of stamps bearing his image in March 1938. His Majesty wore the uniform of an Admiral of the Fleet and, as with the Coronation issue, the stamps were designed and printed in England. The portrait was based on a photograph by well-known English society photographer Dorothy Wilding, who later also provided the image of the next monarch to grace New Zealand's postage stamps, Elizabeth II.

New Zealand's George VI stamp issue began in 1938 with the ½d green, seen here, which was followed by the 1d and 1½d. With wartime postage rate increases, colour changes were made to the lower values, and in July 1941 the ½d stamp was reissued in brown. The 4d and the 9d were issued in 1947. The set was designed by the English printers, while the frame in the pence values—from ½d to 9d—was by William J. Cooch of Wellington.

15 a nation comes of age

1940 centennial

In 1936, four years before the event, New Zealand was already thinking of how it would mark one hundred years of 'organised settlement and government.' At a Centennial Conference in Wellington, the Minister of Internal Affairs, H.E. Parry, suggested that New Zealanders should look to 1940 as their 'national coming-of-age.' He also urged the country to stop 'labouring' the notion of this being a young country. A series of celebrations was planned and the government hoped that every district throughout the dominion would have its own centennial memorial, with its form determined by the local committee.

James Berry's design for the 7d stamp in the Centennial set showed a Maori council taking place on the marae in front of the meeting house. The value, at bottom right, is placed inside the silhouette of a Maori fern-root pounder.

One aspect of the celebrations that could be shared by all New Zealanders was a special set of postage stamps. It was seen as an opportunity to review progress and record important moments in the establishment of British sovereignty in this country. The National Historical Committee provided a

NEW ZEALAND
A MAORI COUNCIL
POSTAGE
7D
& REVENUE
1840 · CENTENNIAL OF NEW ZEALAND · 1940

Opposite: The largest value was also the only vertical format in the 1940 Centennial set. James Berry's 1/- depicted the giant kauri Tane Mahuta, New Zealand's best-known tree.

East Polynesian voyagers struggle ashore in Aotearoa/New Zealand, in the ½d Centennial stamp designed by James Berry.

list of suitable subjects. In the words of the postmaster-general, the themes would 'embrace all aspects of the remarkably full story of the Dominion,' and he was confident the set would be 'one of the finest' yet produced.

Nineteen artists were approached, and the closing date for designs was 30 April 1938. Eleven subjects were prescribed but, as was his habit, James Berry offered an extra one. As a result there were 12 designs in all, the additional one being the five British monarchs who had reigned during the period covered by the centenary. A central portrait of the current king, George VI, was flanked by smaller profiles of his four predecessors, including Edward VIII, whose brief reign meant that he had not yet appeared on a stamp of his own.

Of the 12 Centennial issue designs, nine were provided by Berry and the other three were the work of his colleague and rival, Leonard C. Mitchell. The latter was responsible for the lowest denomination in the set, the ½d Arrival of Maoris in New Zealand 1350. It showed this country's original settlers struggling ashore in a state of physical exhaustion, and resembled another well-known interpretation of this event, the 1899 painting by Charles F. Goldie and Louis J. Steele. Mitchell depicted the Polynesian voyagers arriving with their baskets of kumara, which, according to legend, was planted and flourished in the new environment.

The tradition of wide decorative borders was maintained on most of the Centennial issue. Side panels on the ½d stamp incorporating the tewhatewha, a long-handled Maori weapon whose wooden blade provided a handy location for the denomination. Similarly, A Maori Council was the subject of the 7d stamp (later replaced by an 8d stamp of the same design when the outbreak of war caused an increase in postal rates), in which the denomination was placed inside the form of a Maori fern-root pounder.

The largest value in the set, the 1/-, was designed by Berry and depicted the giant kauri tree Tane Mahuta, from the Waipoua Forest in Northland. The *Centennial News* considered there was no more fitting emblem 'to symbolise the whole period of New Zealand's history' than this, for 'within its life there have been happenings concerning which man can only conjecture.' The tree was believed to have been in existence at the time of the Roman conquest of Britain, and so had witnessed the development of New Zealand 'from a land unknown; it has seen bush and swamp turned to rich

pasture; it has looked unmoving on the trials and triumphs of a young country elevating itself to nationhood.' Some sense of the size of the tree—a sheer 24 m to the first branch—was given by the human figure at the base of the trunk. The subject naturally demanded a vertical format, the only one in the set.

In a departure from previous designs, several Centennial stamps presented combined images. For Captain Cook (1d) and Abel Tasman (2d), James Berry adopted what has been termed both a triptych and tripartite approach, providing a panorama of the navigator, his ship and a chart resulting from his visit to this country. Berry based his drawing of Cook on a bronze statue erected near the Admiralty Arch in London, while his portrait of Tasman was derived from one by J. McDonald in the Alexander Turnbull Library. He also used silhouettes of a Maori wooden handclub as backgrounds for the vital years 1840 and 1940 in the Tasman stamp. The merging effect was also employed by Mitchell on his three-panel The Progress of Transport (4d), illustrating the evolution from the bullock team to railways, steamship and airliner, and achieving what the *Centennial News* described as 'allegorical effect'.

The centennial was a time of reflection and some stamps employed a 'before and after' approach. Berry's 9d stamp contrasted a pair of 1861 gold-panning prospectors with the modern method, the giant gold dredge at Kaniere in north Westland. The Centennial set also recorded single pivotal events in New Zealand history: Berry's Signing of the Treaty of Waitangi (2½d, and based on a bas relief on a monument to Queen Victoria in Cambridge Terrace, Wellington) and Raising of the British Flag at Akaroa (5d), and Mitchell's Landing of Main Body of Immigrants on Petone Beach, Jan. 22nd 1840 (3d), showing new arrivals being greeted by Maori at the settlement then known as Britannia.

In addition to the Centennial stamp designs, the extremely versatile James Berry provided a series of illustrated historic strips for several major newspapers. They were also brought together in a separate and popular publication, *New Zealand in Review*, which coincided with the centennial celebrations and enjoyed numerous editions and reprints.

The new stamps went on sale on 2 January 1940, the day after New Zealanders celebrated the arrival of their centennial year. The *New Zealand*

Opposite: The original artwork (top) for Leonard C. Mitchell's 4d Centennial stamp (bottom) recording the evolution of transport in New Zealand. Restricted to the previous hundred years, this design overlooks the fact that Maori canoes were in service long before bullock teams.

Dutchman Abel Tasman, the first European known to have visited New Zealand, is honoured on James Berry's 2d Centennial stamp. The navigator is shown in three-quarter pose, along with his ship and chart of the west coast of New Zealand.

Herald reported a spirit of 'enthusiastic and hopeful gaiety' by one of the largest such crowds seen in Auckland. An 'amusing interlude' was provided by a young man masquerading as Hitler but his reception was 'to say the least … decidedly mixed.' In Wellington, as the Post Office clock struck midnight to usher in the centennial year, a broadcast message from the Prime Minister, Michael Joseph Savage, was relayed to the street.

The Centennial stamps were intended to be on sale during the period of the national celebrations, but most enjoyed a considerably longer life. An accompanying pamphlet was also issued, to give purchasers—overseas visitors in particular—the historical background to each design. But by the time these stamps had appeared the country was increasingly concerned by developments overseas. The Main Body of the First Echelon—a total of 6520 officers and men—left Wellington for Egypt on 5 January. Among the effects the growing conflict was having at home was a slump in donations and sales of Health stamps, and as a result fewer young New Zealanders were now being sent to health camps.

James Berry's 5d Centennial stamp depicted the raising of the British flag at Akaroa, Banks Peninsula, on 11 August 1840. HMS *Britomart* had been dispatched from the Bay of Islands following rumours of a planned annexation by French settlers, who arrived five days later.

16 back to business

1946 peace

By early May 1945, as the Second World War in Europe drew to an end, the *New Zealand Herald* was finding it something of a struggle to keep up with 'the march (or gallop) of triumph.' Germany surrendered on the 7th and two days later New Zealand celebrated VE (Victory in Europe) Day, which brought out the largest crowds ever seen in Auckland and Christchurch. Rejoicing may have been dampened by knowing that the war in the Pacific was not yet over, but a little more than three months later, after the United States had unleashed nuclear devices on the cities of Hiroshima and Nagasaki, Japan also laid down its arms.

Auckland's VJ (Victory in Japan) Day celebrations on 15 August exceeded those of VE Day as the city 'unashamedly went out and enjoyed itself.' Then it was back to business. In addition to cleaning up after the parties, it was a matter of dismantling air-raid shelters and coastal fortifications, and preparing for the return home of service personnel who were still overseas.

The 1½d value in the 1946 Peace issue, all 11 of which were designed by James Berry, featured St Paul's Cathedral, surrounded by flames and protected by Winston Churchill's defiant 'V for Victory' sign.

NEW ZEALAND
ST. PAULS · LONDON
"THIS WAS THEIR FINEST HOUR"
POSTAGE
REVENUE
1½D.
1½D.

The 1/- and highest value in the 1946 Peace issue depicts the National Memorial Campanile in Wellington.

As early as 1941 the New Zealand Post Office was planning for a Peace stamp issue. In August 1943 a number of artists were invited to submit designs and the final decisions were made in March the following year. James Berry, who had nine out of the 13 designs accepted for the 1940 Centennial issue, now managed the remarkable achievement of having his designs selected for the full set of 11 Peace stamps. This monopoly might be explained by Berry's innate sense of what both the Post Office and the general public wanted. He deliberately offered designs covering several aspects of peace, judging correctly that the war-wearied nation had a hankering for patriotic and sentimental themes ranging from the royal family to the natural scenery of homeland.

New Zealand's first stamps to mark the end of a world war, in 1920, were emblazoned with 'Victory' and images of British lions. The one exception proclaimed 'Peace and Progress' and this was the approach adopted 26 years later. There was hardly an aspect of peace that wasn't mined by Berry, from the placid waters of Lake Matheson seen against a backdrop of the Southern Alps, to the National Memorial Campanile in Wellington. The latter represented the perpetual Light of Remembrance for those who had lost lives in the conflict. The highest value (1/-) and set in a vertical format, this single dominant form mirrored Berry's giant kauri on the Centennial set which was issued six years earlier.

The symbolic lion was now replaced by a knight holding a banner depicting the Cross of St George, the patron saint of England. An echo of Berry's crusader on horse-back on the 1934 Health stamp, this new image had a strong local connection. It was based on a stained-glass window in the Wellington College Memorial Hall, built in the late 1920s in memory of old boys killed in the First World War. The hall has since been demolished.

British royalty was an obvious subject for Berry, and for his 1d design he placed a portrait of George VI in an oval above New Zealand's House of Parliament, a scheme he had offered for a proposed King George V memorial issue a decade earlier. All members of immediate royal family had previously appeared on New Zealand stamps—including princesses Elizabeth and Margaret, on the 1943 and 1944 Health issues—but the 1946 Peace set included the whole family for the first time.

The individual who personified the empire's determination under fire was, of course, British Prime Minister Winston Churchill. Berry proposed him as the subject of a (triangular) design, but regulations did not permit any living person other than members of the royal family to be shown on a stamp. As a result that indomitable spirit was captured by another well-known symbol of London under siege, St Paul's Cathedral, appropriately depicted in red to represent the fires of the Blitz. It was protected by Churchill's signature 'V for Victory' sign and 'This was their finest hour'

British royalty featured on two stamps in New Zealand's 1946 Peace issue. George VI was shown (1d) with New Zealand's Parliament House, Wellington, and also (2d) with members of his immediate family.

NEW ZEALAND
NZ
ONWARD
4d
4d
POSTAGE AND REVENUE

NEW ZEALAND
POSTAGE
REVENUE
5d
5d

from his speech to the House of Commons in June 1940, some five weeks after he had taken over as prime minister.

Berry had introduced the idea of multiple and merged subjects in the 1940 Centennial set and also employed the technique here. In his tributes to the armed forces, he contrasted a tank in a desert with a peaceful New Zealand farm scene, while his acknowledgement of naval achievement balanced the HMNZS *Achilles*—which had taken on the German *Graf Spee* at the Battle of the River Plate—with the *Dominion Monarch*, a well-known passenger liner which also saw war service.

Six weeks before New Zealand's Peace stamps appeared, Australia issued its own set of three. They depicted a seven-pointed star (representing the Australian states and territories), a wreath, the dove of peace on an Australian flag, and—a theme of which Zealandia would have approved—the angel of peace, appearing in a radiant burst of light to figures representing motherhood and industry.

New Zealand's Peace issue proved popular. The *Auckland Star* reported that 'a huge crowd of philatelists, both amateur and professional' had gathered before the doors of the city's Central Post Office opened on the morning of 1 April. Anticipating the heavy demand, three extra clerks were taken on, and during that first morning there were eight queues with about 50 customers in each. But if Aucklanders noticed that all geographic

James Berry's designs for the 1946 Peace issue included tributes to the three armed forces. In the 4d stamp a New Zealand Army badge was flanked with desert warfare and peaceful farming scenes, while the 5d design paired HMNZS *Achilles* and the passenger liner *Dominion Monarch*.

NEW ZEALAND
POSTAGE
REVENUE
9D.
9D.
PEACE
SOUTHERN ALPS FROM CHAPEL WINDOW · WAIHO GORGE

references on the Peace stamps were either to the South Island (Lake Matheson and the Waiho Gorge chapel and Southern Alps) or Wellington (House of Parliament, Campanile and Wellington College window), they would need to get used to it, for the next two commemorative issues would also exclusively feature the South Island.

A month after the issue of New Zealand's 11 Peace stamps, Britain released its own set of two. They took a symbolic approach compared to Berry's highly detailed representations and did not in fact mention the war. Understandably the dominant theme was reconstruction, which was conveyed on one stamp by simple outline drawings of a tractor, houses, a power station and a ship and, on the other, by a set-square, dividers and bricklayer's trowel and bricks. Along with an olive branch and dove of peace they included the obligatory profile of George VI, who made the final selection of the designs after hearing the views of the postmaster-general and the advisory boards.

'A Spirit of Thankfulness' was the descriptive statement James Berry gave to his design for the 9d Peace stamp. It depicted the altar at the chapel at Waiho Gorge, south Westland, with a view through the window to the Franz Joseph Glacier beyond.

17 a message of hope

government life

Prior to becoming New Zealand Premier, Julius Vogel was responsible for one of the first pieces of social legislation passed in this country. The Government Annuities and Life Insurance Bill of 1869 established the Government Life Insurance Office, which offered the prospect of greater security for New Zealanders' dependants—and at an affordable cost. The recent collapse of English insurance companies had prompted the New Zealand Government to enter the business with a scheme which guaranteed annual payments to investors. In February 1870 the Government Life Insurance and Annuity Office opened for business, initially in 13 main centres around the country, which at that stage included Hokitika and Charleston.

As was the practice with other government departments, Government Life had an arrangement with the Post Office to cover the cost of postage on correspondence. But, beginning in late 1888, the two departments had a protracted disagreement over the amount to be paid. This led to the decision

The original artwork and the printed stamp for the 4d value in the 1947 Government Life issue. All eight in this set (the 2½d stamp was released in 1963) were designed by James Berry. The 4d stamp depicted Stephens Island lighthouse, situated at the northern tip of D'Urville Island to guide shipping in Cook Strait.

4d POSTAGE 4d
STEPHENS ISLAND
N Z
GOVERNMENT LIFE
INSURANCE DEPARTMENT

4d POSTAGE 4d
STEPHENS ISLAND
N Z
GOVERNMENT LIFE
INSURANCE DEPARTMENT

N GOVERNMENT Z
LIFE INSURANCE
STATE SECURITY
POSTAGE
ONE PENNY
TWO PENCE
THREE PENCE
HALF PENNY
DEPARTMENT

to allow Government Life to prepay its correspondence by issuing its own stamps. The stamps were required to be of a distinctive design so they couldn't be used for other purposes, while they were also seen as a form of promotion for Government Life.

The original design of Government Life's first stamp was drawn by departmental secretary W. B. Hudson. For a motif he decided on a symbolic lighthouse and may have been inspired by the best-known of all such structures, the Eddystone Light on the Cornish Coast near Plymouth, England. It had been completed only eight years earlier, at a time when New Zealand was beginning to weather the effects of a lengthy economic downturn. Eddystone stood on a solid foundation which could resist waves raised by the fiercest gales and so was an eminently suitably symbol for insurance purposes. It represented an immovable structure and, extending the metaphor, sent out a message of hope to those battered by the storms of economic uncertainty.

The need for real lighthouses was apparent following the organised settlement of New Zealand from Britain. The colony had a heavy dependence on shipping, both local and overseas, which was challenged by a notoriously rugged coastline. It is estimated that to date some 2200 shipwrecks have occurred in these waters, the first recorded instance being in 1795 when the barque *Endeavour*—not to be confused with Captain Cook's vessel—was

The Government Life Office's first stamps, a set of six issued in 1891, depicted a lighthouse radiating 'state security' and the royal reference 'V.R.' The design was by departmental secretary W.B. Hudson and J.F. Rogers of the Government Printing Office. The stamps were reprinted in 1905, when the lighthouse underwent some modifications, and the letters 'V.R.' were removed.

The 1/- and highest value in the 1947 Government Life issue depicted Cape Brett lighthouse in the Bay of Islands.

scuttled in Dusky Sound, Fiordland. The need for a guide for shipping on the eastern headland of Wellington's Harbour, Port Nicholson, was recognised as early as 1840, and so the country's first lighthouse was established on Pencarrow Head in 1859. A second such structure was erected near Nelson in 1862, and by 1881 New Zealand had 21 lighthouses.

The first Government Life Insurance stamps were engraved by A.E. Cousins and went on sale on 2 January 1891. Beams of light radiating from the lighthouse's lantern carried the comforting message 'State Security,' while further assurance was provided by the letters 'V.R.' in a more florid typeface. From 1905 the stamps were reprinted with changes, including the addition of a window to the tower (which was also reduced in height) and the removal of 'V.R.' following the death of Queen Victoria.

Further re-issues of the stamps followed, and in 1945 the Government Life Office began planning an entirely new Pictorial set. James Berry provided designs based on photographs of a selection of New Zealand's lighthouses, while maintaining the historical link by also including the Eddystone Light. Seven stamps were released in 1947 (one more appeared in 1963), and the now 56-year-old symbolic design was replaced by a series of widely varying views of actual structures.

Six of these stamps were overprinted for New Zealand's conversion to decimal currency in 1967, a process which had also engaged James

The original artwork and the printed stamp for the 3d value in the 1947 Government Life issue. It depicts the famous Eddystone Light, near Plymouth, England, the prototype for all modern lighthouses.

The original artwork and the printed stamp for the ½d value in the 1947 Government Life issue, designed by James Berry. The Castlepoint lighthouse, east of Masterton, began operating in 1913.

Berry in another medium. In June 1966, after a protracted competition, he had the satisfaction of learning that his designs had been selected for all six of the planned new circulating coins. He also continued his association with Government Life Insurance with a set of five more lighthouse stamps issued in 1969. They included the Baring Head light (3d), which began operating in 1935 and replaced that on Pencarrow Head, and Dog Island lighthouse in Foveaux Strait. At 36 m the latter was the country's tallest lighthouse and given both a vertical format and the highest (15c) denomination. In 1947 Berry had used minimal borders, but from 1969 (two more earlier designs were issued in 1976), and in keeping with developments in other New Zealand stamps at this time, he did away with them altogether.

The 1976 Government Life stamps were James Berry's last new designs to be issued in New Zealand (there were later issues of his designs in Western Samoa and the Cook Islands). His New Zealand lighthouses had been in service for some 34 years until 1981, when Government Life issued a new set. Designed by Allan Mitchell, they

Beams radiate from two lighthouses in the 1947 Government Life stamp issue, designed by James Berry. Both the Cape Palliser light (2d) and the Brothers light (6d) guide shipping through Cook Strait.

BARING HEAD
3c
N. Z.
GOVERNMENT LIFE
INSURANCE OFFICE

EAST CAPE
8c
N. Z.
GOVERNMENT LIFE
INSURANCE OFFICE

were also a dramatic break with their predecessors. Berry's range of highly detailed pictorial images were replaced by a single graphic representation. It was of no lighthouse in particular and so provided a link with the very first Government Life stamps of 90 years earlier. Mitchell now reduced the image to just four elements—the combined lighthouse and land, sea, sky and the rays from the beacon. The six variations were each printed in three colours (the white of the paper conveniently provided for the lighthouse's rays), in a manner suggestive of a screenprinted multiple by Andy Warhol (p. 217).

In 1989 the Government Life Insurance Corporation became Tower Corporation, a mutual association owned by its policyholders. Because it was no longer a government department it lost its entitlement to issue its own stamps, thereby ending a tradition that was just 15 months short of celebrating its centenary. But true to its name, Tower continued to use its lighthouse logo with its reassuring ray of light. There was another major change at that time, when New Zealand's last lighthouse was 'de-manned' in 1990 and began automatic operation from Wellington.

In 1969, the centenary of the founding of the Government Life Insurance Office, a new series of five stamps was issued. Two more followed in 1976, all designed by James Berry. The 3c 1969 stamp (far left) showed Baring Head light, east of Wellington Harbour; and East Cape light, at the easternmost extremity of the North Island, was on the 8c 1976 stamp (left). The 15c 1969 stamp (above) showed Dog Island lighthouse in Foveaux Strait.

18 pioneering types

provincial centennials

The nation at large celebrated its centennial in 1940, but it was also 100 years since the establishment of European settlements at both Auckland and Wellington. The latter's origins—with the arrival of New Zealand Company settlers at Petone Beach on 22 January 1840—were acknowledged in the Centennial stamp issue, but there was no such stamp to mark Auckland's, on 18 September 1840, when William Hobson raised the British flag near the foreshore. The closest it came was the Centennial set's inclusion of the signing of the Treaty of Waitangi, for after that event Hobson sought a new site for his capital and settled on Auckland.

A lone Maori observes the arrival of the first two immigrant ships at Port Chalmers, Otago, in 1848. Following his clean sweep in the 1946 Peace issue, James Berry also designed all four stamps in the Otago Centennial set in 1948.

Several parts of the country could claim European connections predating 1840. The oldest surviving such settlement still in existence is Kerikeri in the Bay of Islands, which was founded in 1819 but had to wait until 1969, when it was 150 years old, before it was acknowledged on a postage stamp. Nearby Kororareka, later renamed Russell, was already well-known to shipping by

NEW ZEALAND
POSTAGE
REVENUE
THE "JOHN WICKLIFFE"
AND "PHILIP LAING" AT
PORT CHALMERS-1848
1D.
1D.
CENTENNIAL OF OTAGO

A vertical format was demanded for First Church Dunedin, in the Otago Centennial issue of 1948. James Berry's design emphasises the province's origins with a Scotch thistle.

the 1830s. A boisterous town, it had a reputation as the 'Hell-hole of the Pacific.' In all respects it preceded organised settlement of this country, and it was the generally lawless nature of the Bay of Islands that eventually prompted the British Government to colonise New Zealand.

In 1948 Otago became the first province to have its own centennial marked by a special issue of stamps. Although Europeans were in the region by the 1830s, attracted by the local stocks of seals and whales, Otago officially began with the arrival at Port Chalmers of the immigrant ship *John Wickliffe* on 23 March 1848, followed by the *Philip Laing* three weeks later. All four Otago stamps were designed by James Berry, who was also responsible for the province's centennial medal. Like his 1d stamp, this depicted the arrival of the first ships and a Maori observer. Following the style of his earlier Centennial and Peace issues, the stamps were highly detailed and three had decorative borders. The old and the new were contrasted with a ghostly stage-coach and horses appearing over a view of the town of Cromwell, whose beginnings were stimulated by the discovery of gold. Two stamps emphasised architectural achievement in the form of Otago University (the first to be founded in New Zealand) and Dunedin's First Church, which was closely associated with the original scheme to settle Otago.

Nearly three years later, the Canterbury Centennial stamps followed a similar format. That province also had Europeans from the mid-1830s, and

French settlers at Akaroa in 1840 (which prompted the HMS *Britomart* to be dispatched there to raise the British flag, an event included in the 1940 Centennial issue). But it was the arrival of four immigrant ships at Lyttelton in December 1850 that marked Canterbury's official beginnings. The original plan was for four stamps in the set, but following complaints that the province extended some distance beyond Christchurch, it was decided to include a view of Timaru to acknowledge South Canterbury.

The stamps included tributes to the pioneer women who trudged over the Port Hills to their new home, and to John Robert Godley, founder of Canterbury. In designs by James Berry, two local landmarks, the Christchurch Cathedral and Canterbury University, were placed within decorative arched borders reflecting the distinctive neo-gothic architecture. But three days after the stamps were released, in November 1950, the first of a number of complaints was published in the *Christchurch Press.* Correspondents pointed out that the set ignored Lyttelton, where the Canterbury pioneers had first landed on New Zealand soil, and that the colours were 'washed-out.' Further, the representation of Christchurch Cathedral was compared unfavourably with that of Dunedin's First Church in the Otago issue. W.A. (Bill) Sutton, artist and teacher at the Canterbury School of Art, entered the debate. With the exception of the Godley stamp (designed by J.A. Johnstone, also on the staff of the School of Art), which he considered 'an excellent

John Robert Godley, Chief Agent of the Canterbury Association, was honoured in that province's Centennial issue of 1950. Designed by J.A. Johnstone; the four others in the set were by James Berry (3) and Leonard C. Mitchell (1).

James Berry took advantage of arching trees to frame Canterbury University College (now the University of Canterbury) in that province's Centennial stamp issue of 1950.

The first Europeans to come to Southland were attracted by whales. The drama of a hunt in Foveaux Strait was the subject of this design, by E.R. Leeming, for the Southland Centennial issue of 1956.

Presumed extinct until rediscovered in 1948, this sideface takahe was given the highest value (8d) in the Southland Centennial set of 1956. Designed by M.R. Smith.

stamp marred by awkward engraving,' Sutton found the set 'uninspired'. He suggested the matter might be settled if the proposed stamps were submitted for comment by the heads of design at leading art schools in London and Edinburgh. He was informed that the New Zealand postal authorities had been advised by committees, one of which had included the director of the Canterbury School of Art.

The South Island also provided the next province to mark its centennial with postage stamps. Southland was officially founded in 1856 with the setting out of Invercargill but, once again, there had been earlier European settlements, as at Riverton in the mid-1830s. The province's three stamps were all by different artists, resulting in distinctive designs but a lack of unity in the set. Two were panoramic tributes to the important early industries of whaling (designed by E.R. Leeming) and farming (by Leonard C. Mitchell), the latter showing a local equivalent of Ceres, the Roman goddess of agriculture and grain, with a cow and sheep. By comparison, the third (8d) stamp (designed by

M.R. Smith) had as its single focus the first bird to be seen on a New Zealand stamp for 21 years. It honoured the takahe, which was believed to have been extinct for 50 years until rediscovered in the Murchison Mountains in Fiordland by Dr Geoffrey Orbell in 1948. The bird's reappearance was a bright spot for New Zealand during a period of deteriorating industrial relations and growing concern for military developments in Asia. And while the other stamps in the Southland set appeared to dwell on the past, the right-facing takahe was seen striding confidently into the future.

Three more sets of provincial centennials followed, with Hawke's Bay (1958), Marlborough (1959) and Westland (1960) producing a total of nine stamps. But in contrast to earlier such issues, James Berry now provided only one design, for the (3d) view of Cape Kidnappers in the Hawke's Bay set, although he was responsible for the 1958 Health stamps. Another significant change to New Zealand's stamps during that decade was the final shrugging off of the heavy decorative frames of the past.

The Roman goddess Ceres is accompanied by a cooperative cow and sheep in Leonard C. Mitchell's tribute to farming in Southland.

19 returning to normality

post-war health

In the decade prior to the Second World War, James Berry's designs were accepted for five issues of New Zealand's Health stamps. But from 1943 until 1958, when his last such stamp was accepted, he dominated the field, providing designs for 10 of the 16 issues. Of the six not by him, three were sourced from England while the others were by Leonard C. Mitchell and another Wellington artist, E. Mervyn Taylor.

Because of war conditions, the same design was used for the Health stamps of 1939 and 1940 and again the following year when it was simply overprinted with '1941'. It was designed by S. Hall of the Post and Telegraph Department, and based on photographs of boys playing with a ball in Wellington. The theme of young New Zealanders at play was continued in 1942 when the same designer now provided a pair of Wellingtonians on a swing. Then, after a pause of four years, James Berry was back, with a slight change of subject and a very different format. His depictions of the young

Returning to civilian duties, a New Zealander in uniform assists a young girl over a stile. James Berry's 1946 Health stamp is rich in symbolism, with the child being put on the path to health and happiness. Behind the pair, coastal fortifications and barbed wire refer to the recent war.

NEW ZEALAND
POSTAGE
1D.
HEALTH
1/2D.

This design, by S. Hall and the Wellington Post and Telegraph Department, first appeared on Health stamps in 1939. An increase in postal charges before they were issued required them to be overprinted, 1d and 2d respectively. War conditions resulted in the same design being used again in 1940, although they were now printed (as opposed to overprinted) with the increased postal rates. As the war continued, existing stocks of the 1940 stamp, plus a small additional printing, were overprinted '1941' for that year's Health stamp.

princesses Margaret and Elizabeth were the first official triangular stamps issued by this country, and the only such examples of this shape until New Zealand Post marked the centenary of the (unofficial) Pigeongram stamps in 1997. Berry's 1943 designs were also innovative in that they were the first Health stamps to both show particular people and members of the royal family. The triangular format may have given the stamps some novelty value—as well as some difficulty in separating them—but the subject of young royals during wartime proved immensely popular with the patriotic public.

The triangular Health stamps were issued on 1 October 1943, at a time when New Zealand forces were in action in Italy and the Pacific, and there was debate at home as to whether married men who had served overseas should be required to return to duty. Such developments were referred to at the official launch of the stamps by the Governor-General, Sir Cyril Newall: 'We are fighting this, the greatest war known to history, in order that our children shall receive from our hands the heritage which we hold in trust for them.' He also advised there were now 16 permanent health camps in New Zealand, although three had been requisitioned for military purposes.

The two princesses reappeared on the following year's Health stamps, which reverted to a more conventional rectangular format. Reflecting the

New Zealand's first official triangular format, James Berry's 1943 Health stamp stamps showed the young princesses, Margaret and Elizabeth.

Princesses Elizabeth (as a Sea Ranger) and Margaret (Girl Guide) on the 1944 Health stamp, designed by James Berry.

spirit of the times, the royal sisters were shown in uniform, with Elizabeth as a Sea Ranger and Margaret as a Girl Guide. These stamps, designed in England and based on photographs by Dorothy Wilding, had a strong New Zealand reference with a border of kowhai flowers and also proved extremely popular with the public.

After a succession of young New Zealanders and royals, Health stamps adopted a more symbolic approach in 1945. James Berry's design showed the statue of Peter Pan from Kensington Gardens London, representing immortal youth. It was the country's only new postage stamp issued that year and appeared seven months before the cessation of hostilities in Europe. This country would soon begin the process of rebuilding and returning to normality, the inspiration for James Berry's 1946 design showing a soldier in uniform helping a young girl over a stile. The symbolism continued with the following year's stamp, another by Berry and an echo of his earlier Peter Pan. The statue of Eros, in London's Piccadilly Circus, was a tribute to Victorian philanthropist and factory reformer Lord Shaftsbury, who had campaigned for the welfare of children.

The next decade saw Health issues return to their earlier interest in local subjects and outdoor activities. Yacht racing was the theme in 1951 stamp, by Berry and R.S. Phillips of Rangiora, and leading the field was a New Zealand-designed Takapuna class boat, appropriately named *Health*. The message was reinforced with a device Berry had used on his 1933 Pathway to Health, the beneficial rays of the sun radiating from the top right-hand corner. These stamps were issued on 1 November 1951, and the campaign was launched by Auckland Mayor Sir John Allum. The Highland Dancing Society formed a guard of honour on the steps of the Central Post Office, while eager customers were served at 12 special counters and an outside booth. Reflecting the nautical theme of the stamps, Allum describe the proceeds from their sale as 'the sheet anchor of the health camp movement' and one which had paid for the maintenance of 600 children during the previous year. It was New Zealand's 23rd issue of Health stamps, and the aim was to raise £110,000 before the stamps were withdrawn from sale in January. Sales certainly got off to a good start, with the Auckland postal district managing a record £10,937, which was £2294 up on the previous year's figure. Taupo also managed to break its previous record of £108 by selling £142 worth. The appearance of the 1951 stamps coincided with the announcement that the country's largest health camp, at Pakuranga, was now complete and could accommodate 100 needy Auckland children during

The statue of Eros in London's Piccadilly Circus, a memorial to Victorian philanthropist Lord Shaftsbury, was the subject of the 1947 Health stamp, designed by James Berry.

Leonard C. Mitchell's design for the 1956 Health stamps was based on a photograph of children playing in an orchard. Presumably apples were chosen because of their claim to 'keep the doctor away'!

Opposite: The Takapuna class yacht *Health* leading the field, assisted by the health-giving rays of the sun. The 1951 Health stamp, designed by James Berry, and R.S. Phillips of Rangiora.

the year plus an additional 50 during the summer holidays.

Further to the young princesses in the early 1940s, Health stamps now had a new generation of royal subjects to consider. These began with Princess Elizabeth and her first child, Prince Charles, on the 1950 stamp, which was another collaboration between James Berry and R.S. Phillips. Two years later, and in anticipation of their parents' visit to New Zealand, Prince Charles and his younger sister Princess Anne were featured on the 1952 English-designed Health stamps.

NEW ZEALAND
HEALTH
1D.
Z 1
HEALTH
2D. POSTAGE
& REVENUE

A young tramper confronts the challenge of Mt Aspiring on the 1954 Health stamp (right), by James Berry. The last Health stamps to be designed by him were the 1954 issue, depicting the Girls' Life Brigade (left) and Boys' Brigade.

There was also a reference to the princesses of 1944 with Berry's 1953 Health stamp, which marked the 30th anniversary of the formation of the Girl Guides Association and also acknowledged Boy Scouts. While decorative borders had long since disappeared, these two stamps were distinguished by having the word 'Health' spelt out on their top edges in the dots and dashes of morse code, a signalling method familiar to Guides and Scouts. Another healthy outdoor activity was the theme for the next year's stamp, also by Berry. He presented a young tramper contemplating the appropriately named Mt Aspiring, while the background acknowledged a greater challenge, the conquering of Mt Everest some 16 months earlier by New Zealander Sir Edmund Hillary and the Nepalese Sherpa Tenzing.

Berry's Guides and Scouts pairing of 1953 set a precedent for two other uniformed youth organisations, Boys' and Girls' Brigade, which were recognised in 1958, and were his last accepted Health designs. Health stamps then underwent changes in both subject and approach. They would occasionally return to royal themes, as with Prince Andrew in 1963, but from 1959 they moved into areas that had previously been the exclusive preserve of the definitive sets, beginning with native birds.

Symbolising immortal youth, the statue of Peter Pan in London's Kensington Gardens was the subject of the 1945 Health stamp, designed by James Berry.

20 royal visitors

Elizabeth II

The first member of the British Royal family to visit New Zealand was Prince Alfred, Duke of Edinburgh, who came here in 1869-70 as Captain of the Royal Navy steam frigate HMS *Galatea*. He was Queen Victoria's second son and did not become king, unlike the next royal visitors to these shores. The Duke and Duchess of Cornwall and York (later King George V and Queen Mary) and the Prince of Wales (later King Edward VIII) came in 1901 and 1920 respectively, to personally thank New Zealand for its support of the empire during the war in South Africa and the First World War. But of the reigns of George VI and Edward VIII, only the former was marked by the issue of a stamp in New Zealand (pp. 122–129).

New Zealand's first Definitive Elizabeth II series was issued on 1 March 1954 and consisted of stamps in three sizes. The middle size, covering values from ½d to 1/9, were designed by Leonard C. Mitchell.

New Zealand had not yet hosted a reigning monarch, but a visit by King George VI, Queen Elizabeth and Princess Margaret in 1949 was planned. James Berry provided designs for a set of stamps but the tour had to be abandoned on account of the king's health. The stamps were

EIIR
1s
NEW ZEALAND

New Zealand issued a series of five Coronation stamps on 25 May 1953, a week before the event at Westminster Abbey. James Berry designed the 2d Buckingham Palace and 8d Westminster Abbey, while Leonard C. Mitchell was responsible for the 1/6 Crown and Royal Sceptre.

altered in anticipation of a visit in 1952, but that was also cancelled. One of the necessary changes was the ship that would bring the royal party; now MV *Gothic*, not HMS *Vanguard*. A third visit, and now by Princess Elizabeth and Prince Philip, was planned for 1953 but that was also cancelled because of the king's illness. Finally, in late 1953 New Zealand received its first visit by a reigning monarch.

Queen Elizabeth II had featured on previous New Zealand stamps. As Princess Elizabeth she was depicted on the Peace issue of 1946 (p. 141), and the Health issues of 1943, 1944 and 1950 (pp. 167 & 168). Her next appearance was on three of the five stamps issued to mark her Coronation at Westminster Abbey on 2 June 1953 (pp. 174–181). James Berry dominated the set with four designs, two being large and detailed views of Buckingham Palace and the state coach with the queen's head in an oval. His two other contributions were smaller and simpler, showing a profile of the queen and the façade of Westminster Abbey. Leonard C. Mitchell designed the largest denomination in the set (1/6), depicting the crown and royal sceptre.

On 23 December 1953 the Queen and Duke of Edinburgh arrived at Auckland on SS *Gothic*. During their stay in New Zealand they visited 46 towns and cities and attended 110 separate functions, from Waitangi to Invercargill. In all their journey involved some 2100 kilometres of travel by car, 1160 by air and 970 by train, before they left the country from Bluff on

One of the two stamps—both designed by Leonard C. Mitchell—issued on 9 December 1953 in anticipation of the visit to New Zealand by Elizabeth II and the Duke of Edinburgh.

One of Leonard C. Mitchell's 1953 Royal Visit stamps showed both the queen and the Duke of Edinburgh. It would be the duke's only appearance on a New Zealand stamp until the Golden Wedding issue in 1997.

30 January 1954. The arrival of the royal entourage was marked by the release of a pair of stamps, both designed by Leonard C. Mitchell and distinguished by tapering Maori borders on two sides. They presented the queen both singly and with the Duke of Edinburgh, but neither stamp had the impact of the previous Coronation set.

The royal visit coincided with the issue of the first of the Queen Elizabeth II Definitive stamps, to replace those depicting the late King George VI. These came in three different sizes according to denomination. Because there was decreasing need for stamps for duty payments, the words 'postage and revenue'—which had appeared on all New Zealand stamps (except Health issues)—were no longer required. Altogether there were 16 values in the set and, not surprisingly, the successful designers were Leonard C. Mitchell (responsible for values from ½d to 8d and 9d to 1/9) and James Berry (values from 2/6 to 10/-). For the lower values Mitchell produced a left-facing three-quarter profile of the queen based on a 1952 photograph (which was also used for on Britain's first Elizabeth II stamps) by Dorothy Wilding. Her Majesty wore the diamond diadem made for George IV in the 1820s. This had been worn by Queen Victoria for all her appearances on British stamps, including the first Penny Black.

The values from ½d to 8d appeared in one colour, while those from 9d to 1/6—showing a right-facing three-quarter profile—were slightly larger and printed in two colours. For the four largest values, from 2/6 to 10/-, Berry provided an illustration of the queen in the uniform of the Grenadier Guards, on horseback in preparation for the Trooping the Colour ceremony. The smaller values in the set included two local references: a kowhai flower in the top left corner balanced by the four stars of the Southern Cross at the bottom right. But as a result of complaints that the denominations were too small, and that several stamps were too similar in colour, the set was redrawn. The seven new stamps, which began appearing from October 1955, were given more distinct colours, and while the kowhai was retained, the Southern Cross was eliminated to allow for larger denominations.

In an article in the 1951 *Year Book of the Arts in New Zealand*, artist Eric Lee-Johnson had been extremely critical of the standard of this country's stamp design. On the treatment of royal heads he quoted Fritz Hellmut Ehmcke, an influential German typographer and book designer in the 1920s: 'It is wisest for such a portrait to be stamped in profile, and thus removed from the sphere of everyday appearances.' Previously, monarchs on New Zealand stamps had appeared variously in full face, three-quarter and profile poses, and Berry opted for the latter when he provided yet another Queen Elizabeth II design, the 1954 Official set for government

The four highest values in the Elizabeth II Definitive set—from 2/6 to 10/-—were designed by James Berry and showed the queen on horseback.

The lower values in the Elizabeth II definitive set were designed by Leonard C. Mitchell and were issued from late 1953. Following criticism that the denominations were too small (4d, left), the stamps were redrawn and issued from 1955. The figures were enlarged, while the Southern Cross was removed (2d and 4d, centre and right).

Opposite: James Berry's design for the 1954 Elizabeth II Official set presented a sideface portrait of the queen against a background of the letters 'N' and 'Z'.

departmental use. In a break with tradition, Her Majesty was now right-facing and given local context with a background pattern composed of the letters 'N' and 'Z'.

Elizabeth II has continued to make regular appearances on New Zealand stamps, marking both the country's celebrations (stamp centennial, 1955, and New Zealand Day, 1974) and her own anniversaries (silver jubilee, 1977, and golden wedding, 1997). If she reigns until 10 September 2015 she will become the longest-reigning British monarch in history, surpassing the 63 years and 216 days her great-grandmother Queen Victoria spent on the throne. Unless New Zealand decides to become a republic in the meantime, that occasion will surely be an excuse for another set of Elizabeth II stamps.

OFFICIAL
1s
NEW ZEALAND
1s
OFFICIAL
9d
NEW ZEALAND
9d

21 carrying the mail

Stamp centennial

Painter and photographer Eric Lee-Johnson had been critical of New Zealand stamp design, so he may have held out little hope for the planned Stamp Centennial issue in 1955. Two years earlier, when a competition for entries was announced, he complained that previous judging panels had been 'top-heavy with officials and philatelists with no special knowledge of design.' That, he explained in a letter to the *New Zealand Herald*, was why 'leading professional designers' did not take part. There was also the 'niggardly size of the awards'—'the meagre prize of £50' offered for accepted designs.

On 18 July 1955 the exact centenary of the release of New Zealand's first stamps was marked by a commemorative issue celebrating postal progress. Presumably Eric Lee-Johnson approved of one of the three designs being a modern interpretation of the country's first stamp, which he had previously described as 'hold[ing] its own among the better of the early Colonials,

A mail-carrying DC-3 designed by Allan Mitchell, the highest value (4d) in the 1955 Stamp Centennial set.

1855 - 1955
NAC
NEW ZEALAND
NEW ZEALAND 4D

Elizabeth II echoing the pose of her great-grandmother Queen Victoria on the original Full Face. The 3d value, designed by James Berry, in the 1955 Stamp Centennial set.

Opposite: The original artwork (left) by R. Maurice Conly for the 2d Maori mail runner (right) in the 1955 Stamp Centennial set.

and others issued before the turn of the century.'

The new stamp was designed by James Berry, and depicted Elizabeth II in a similar three-quarter pose (although facing right instead of left) to that of Victoria in the 1855 Full Faces, and wearing the same diadem (crown) and sash. But a more recent commentator, Laurie Franks, was unimpressed by this modern version, finding it 'uninspired' and with 'the insipid appearance of the Royal Visit stamps.' He also suggested a stronger colour might have improved matters.

The other two stamps in the set contrasted ancient and modern methods of mail-carrying and were innovative in that they introduced movement. Apart from the outdoors activities that had been regular features of Health issues, New Zealand stamps had remained decidedly static, and previous depictions of aircraft and ships, for example, had been constrained by their borders and surroundings.

The 2d Stamp Centennial design, by R. Maurice Conly, recorded the original overland method of mail transportation around this country. Postal routes were established soon after the beginning of organised European settlement and in 1843 a twice-monthly service began between Auckland and Wellington, via Kawhia and New Plymouth. The route lay almost entirely along the coast, a distance of about 700 km, and the service took an average of three weeks. Such journeys depended largely on the assistance

NEW ZEALAND
1855
1955
TWO PENCE

NEW ZEALAND
1855
1955
TWO PENCE

of the various tribes through whose territory the mail passed, and Maori mail-carriers were noted for providing an extremely reliable service.

The early loads borne by Maori mail-carriers were upwards of a hefty 34 kg, but by the late 1850s had been reduced to a much more reasonable 12 kg. However, it seems that Conly's postal courier was not carrying anything like this weight in the kete over his shoulder. He wore a flax skirt and cape, and was placed in a recognisable Auckland landscape with a background of Rangitoto and ships in the harbour. These distant details rather gave the sense that the barefoot runner was something of a giant, who also had to avoid the lettering overhead.

Human effort was superseded by technological progress on the largest (4d) denomination stamp in the set, designed by Allan Mitchell. This presented the most modern method of mail-carrying in New Zealand at the time, the DC-3 aircraft. It had been developed in the United States in the mid-1930s, and went into service in New Zealand in 1948. It dominated the NAC fleet throughout the 1950s and its last scheduled service with that airline was in 1973. The DC-3 was not the first aircraft to be shown on a New Zealand stamp but earlier planes were reduced to decorative elements, whereas this DC-3 had a real sense of movement. In the spirit of the age it was given a streamlined background and it was definitely a case of onwards and upwards.

Reproductions of the first Full Face Queens of 1855 marked the 125th anniversary of the first New Zealand postage stamps in 1980. Designed by D.A. Hatcher, Auckland.

14c
125TH. ANNIVERSARY
FIRST STAMP ISSUE · 1980
New Zealand
NEW ZEALAND
POSTAGE
ONE PENNY
14c
125TH. ANNIVERSARY
FIRST STAMP ISSUE · 1980
New Zealand
NEW ZEALAND
POSTAGE
TWO PENCE

In 1980, a quarter-century after the Stamp Centennial, the 125th anniversary provided an opportunity to showcase the original Full Faces. In a design by Don A. Hatcher, the 1d, 2d and 1/- values from 1855 were reproduced 'se tenant', meaning that the three different stamps were printed together on the same sheet, while another difference was their adjustment to then-current postal rates of 14 cents. This trio was part of a set which included three other 1980 events, all designed by R. Maurice Conly: the centenary of Rotorua, an international orchid conference in Auckland and the World Ploughing Championships at Lincoln Agricultural College. Then in 1988 the Chalon portrait that was the basis of the original Full Faces was reproduced on a $1 stamp as part of the Royal Philatelic Society of New Zealand's centennial set. It was accompanied by two 40c designs which compared a profile of Elizabeth II with that of Victoria on the Second Sidefaces of 1882.

The 150th anniversary of New Zealand's first adhesive postage stamp in 2005 was a major affair. Postal history was acknowledged with the release of reproductions of 15 earlier stamps in groups to represent the three half-centuries to date. The first naturally included a Full Face Queen, as well as an 1873 Sideface and the 1901 Universal Postage stamp, while the Red Boy represented Health stamps in the second group. The final set of five included the 50th anniversary of the Anzac landing at Gallipoli in 1965 and the round kiwi design of 1990. That symbolic bird was recognised as 'the obvious—and perhaps the only acceptable' image for this country's first round stamp. And in the words of New Zealand Post, our philatelic heritage would be incomplete without a tribute to 'our world-famous sporting heroes—the indomitable All Blacks,' so this last selection also included the 2003 stamp marking 100 years of New Zealand test rugby.

As previously noted, if Queen Elizabeth II attains the age of 89 years in 2015 she will become the longest reigning monarch in British history. That same year will also mark the 160th anniversary of New Zealand's first stamps and no doubt provide a further opportunity for celebration. In which case our pioneering Full Face Queens may make yet another reappearance.

To mark the 125th anniversary of the first New Zealand stamps, in 1980 New Zealand Post issued three 14c stamps showing reproductions of the original Full Face Queens.

22 national institutions

plunket & sheep

For the first 80 years, the only identifiable portraits found on New Zealand stamps were those of British monarchs. There was a small and extremely indistinct depiction of Captain Cook in the 1906 Christchurch Exhibition issue but the first real break with tradition came when the 1935 Pictorial set included a recognisable likeness of the great navigator. Five years later, the Centennial issue also included Cook, along with Abel Tasman, while the next non-royal to be so honoured was John Robert Godley, founder of Canterbury, in 1950.

It was not until 1957 that a New Zealand-born individual was shown on one of this country's stamps. First to receive this distinction was Frederick Truby King, who had been born in Taranaki in 1858. He grew up in Nelson, and after studying medicine in Edinburgh he returned to New Zealand and worked at the Seacliff Mental Hospital near Dunedin. His concern for child welfare led to the formation of the Society for the Promotion of Health of

Droving a flock of Southdown sheep and, at top left, a sideface portrait of a lamb. One of a set of five stamps, designed by Leonard C. Mitchell, marking the Chamber of Commerce Empire Conference in Wellington in 1936.

NEW ZEALAND
2½D
CHAMBER OF COMMERCE EMPIRE CONFERENCE WELLINGTON OCT·1936
POSTAGE & REVENUE

A full face portrait of Sir Truby King, on the 1957 3d stamp marking the 50th anniversary of the founding of the Plunket Society.

Women and Children, later known as the Plunket Society as a result of the support it received from Lady Plunket, wife of the then Governor of New Zealand. Truby King opened a home for under-nourished babies at Karitane, north of Dunedin, and that name was applied to the Plunket Society's baby hospitals which were established throughout the country. Their trained staff were known as Karitane nurses, while Karitane was also the brand-name for an infant food.

Truby King was knighted in 1925, and when he died in 1938 he became this country's first private citizen to be given a state funeral. According to the *Dictionary of New Zealand Biography* he was independent-minded, impatient with bureaucracy, careless with money, and cared little for the state of his clothes. Those characteristics may not be apparent in his postal portrait on a 1957 stamp, designed by M. R. Smith of Levin, marking the 50th anniversary of the founding of Plunket. It was based on a photograph which is held in the New Zealand Post Archive, with a note: 'This photograph shows paralysis of the eye muscles and a deformed shoulder, which have been corrected in the design.'

Aside from the obligatory Health issues, New Zealand issued only two other stamps in 1957 and both honoured another national institution—sheep. There had been previous references to the animal in both the 1936 Chamber of Commerce set and the Southland Centennial set of 1956, but neither was such a direct celebration as that of 1957. And in terms of effectiveness of design, these two stamps were in sharp contrast to the Plunket stamp which followed three months later.

A truckload of bales makes its way from the farm to the wool store in the city, while an inset shows a shearer at work. The lowest value in the 1936 Chamber of Commerce set, designed by Leonard C. Mitchell.

This pair of sheep stamps marked what has been recognised as the single most important event in the history of the New Zealand economy, the country's first successful shipment of frozen meat to the United Kingdom. They were issued 75 years to the day after the departure from Port Chalmers, on 15 February 1882, of the *Dunedin*, which historian Gavin McLean has described as '[t]he ship that changed our destiny.' Its precious cargo, of 4311 carcasses of mutton, 598 of lamb, 22 pork and 2226 sheeps' tongues, arrived in good order, apart from one single carcass which had been 'bumped'. All were sold, receiving excellent prices at London's Smithfield Market. Although some of the sheep had been frozen for over four months, it was said to look like freshly killed mutton. The shipment's successful arrival in London was described by *The*

A sheep poses with the ships, past and present, that have taken its frozen meat to Britain. Designed by Michael Goaman to mark the 75th anniversary of New Zealand's lamb export trade in 1957.

Opposite: A sheep astride New Zealand, in the 4d stamp marking the 75th anniversary of the lamb export trade in 1957. Designed by Michael Goaman.

Times as a 'prodigious feat' and even received a favorable mention in the House of Lords.

The *Dunedin* was soon followed by other ships, leading to the establishment of freezing works throughout New Zealand. By 1889 the number of carcasses exported exceeded one million, while the nature of the national flock changed to suit the taste of English consumers. In 1894 the *New Zealand Official Year Book* could refer to 'that most valuable of animals—the sheep.'

The two 1957 stamps were by the Englishman Michael Goaman who, with his wife Sylvia, was responsible for stamps designs for over 40 countries. The hallmark of a Goaman design was legibility and strong visual impact, and the sheep of New Zealand were well-served on both counts. One stamp depicted the animal astride an outline map of the country, with one foot on the West Coast of the South Island and the tail somewhere in the Wairarapa. The other presented it alongside profiles of the *Dunedin* and its modern refrigerated equivalent. Both stamps benefitted from simple uncluttered designs with integrating images and lettering set against plain border-free backgrounds.

On the 75th anniversary of refrigerated shipping in 1957 the *New Zealand Herald* observed: 'On the rolling pasture lands of New Zealand graze

40 million sheep and six million cattle, the living structure upon which has been built one of the richest rural economies in the world.' At that stage New Zealand was Britain's main supplier of meat, ahead of Argentina, Denmark and Australia. Meat represented 25 percent of this country's export income. As part of the celebrations marking the release of the two new stamps, a special post office opened for that day only at Totara, just south of Oamaru, where the first meat had been prepared for shipment back in 1882.

The full centennial of the export of refrigerated meat was marked by a much less impressive single stamp in 1982. Nine years later the sheep of New Zealand had an issue to themselves, acknowledging six different breeds developed to provide particular types of wool and meat. The Romney, which arrived in this country in 1853 and came to dominate the national flock, was naturally selected for the highest denomination stamp ($1.80) in the set, designed by Lindy Fisher of Auckland. But by now the sheep of New Zealand were experiencing other challenges, beyond the shearing shed and freezing works. Government subsidies had encouraged the country's flock numbers to skyrocket, reaching an all-time high of 70.3 million in mid-1982. But in the interests of a more efficient economy, such protectionism could not be sustained, and the removal of subsidies had a dramatic effect. By mid-1989 the national sheep population was down to 60.6 million and still dropping, but has since levelled off at around 39 million.

23 symbolic birds

kiwi

On the morning of 17 January 1770 the *Endeavour* was about a quarter of a mile offshore in Queen Charlotte Sound at the north-eastern corner of the South Island. Captain James Cook and his men were the first Europeans to enter this part of New Zealand and to report on the astonishing birdlife. Botanist Joseph Banks noted in his journal that he had been awakened by the singing of the birds: '[T]he numbers of them were certainly very great who seemd to strain their throats with emulation perhaps; their voices were certainly the most melodious wild musick I have ever heard, almost imitating small bells but with the most tunable silver sound imaginable to which the distance was no small addition … they begin to sing about 1 or 2 in the morn and continue till sunrise, after which they are silent all day like our nightingales.'

The kiwi was chosen for New Zealand's first round postage stamp in 1988, designed by Allan Mitchell. The stamp first appeared in green, and was later printed in red (1991), blue (1993), purple (1997) and gold (2000).

Despite the volume of that dawn chorus, New Zealand has far fewer species of birds than other countries such as Britain and Australia, a

ONE DOLLAR
$1
NEW ZEALAND

For its first postal outing, in the 1898 Pictorials, the 6d Kiwi was printed in green. The same design, by E. Howard, reappeared in 1900, and the colour was changed to red.

Opposite: The 1935 Pictorials included this profile of a kiwi, its symbolic status enhanced by the four stars of the Southern Cross. Designed by C.H. and R.J.G Collins.

result of its long separation from any other land mass. But those same conditions also provided a predator-free environment, which encouraged the development of a large number of flightless birds, among them the kiwi and extinct moa.

When the call went out in 1895 for suitable designs for New Zealand's first set of Pictorial postage stamps, it was to be expected that several birds would be put forward. The local ornithology was represented by three in the final set of 13 stamps: a pair of huia (3d) (p. 26), a kiwi (6d) and a kea and a kaka (1/-) (p. 27). But it was something of an inauspicious beginning, for in real life the huia was under threat as a result of the decorative use of its tail feathers. It became extinct around 1907. For its postal debut the kiwi was represented by an oddly proportioned and rather scruffy specimen and, as with its feathered colleagues, was crowded in by an overly decorative border. The pairing of the kea and kaka was also unusual because those two birds frequented vastly different natural habitats: the kea lived among the snow and rocks of the high country, while the kaka preferred the trees of the forest. The images of the huia and of the kea and kaka were based on paintings by the Dutch ornithological artist J.G. Keulemans. They were originally produced for Walter Buller's magnificent book *The Birds of New Zealand*, which was published in 1888. Keuleman's birds also had other applications and were well-known to young New Zealanders when reproduced on the covers of school pads in the 1950s.

In the 1890s the first kiwi stamp underwent several changes. It went from green to red and, along with the two other Pictorial bird stamps, was reduced in size for consistency and more economical printing. With the onset of the First World War, the real kiwi now began to cement its claim as unofficial national symbol and would soon give its name to New Zealanders at large. This association was recognised in 1935 with the 1d Kiwi stamp (designed by C.H. and R.J.G. Collins), one of a trio of native birds in the country's second pictorial issue. Compared to the earlier kiwi, this was a much sleeker specimen with clearly visible whiskers, although there were suggestions that it appeared unstable and was about to topple on its beak. The bird was presented symbolically, in profile, and surrounded by elements representative of New Zealand. It foraged beneath a cabbage tree, but was constrained by an ornate frame of Maori carvings, fern and the Southern Cross. The other two birds accompanying the kiwi in the Second Pictorial set were the fantail, or piwakwaka (½d), and tui (1/-).

Remarkably, another two decades would pass before the next appearance on a local postage stamp of a New Zealand bird: the flightless takahe as part of the Southland Centennial set of 1956. Two years later another protected native bird, the gannet and its nesting grounds at Cape Kidnappers, took the largest stamp (designed by James Berry) in the Hawke's Bay Centennial set. Then in 1959 the kiwi returned in support of the Pan-Pacific Boy Scouts Jamboree held at Auckland's Cornwall Park. It had the distinction of being the first New Zealand stamp to be designed by a woman, Shirley M. Collins, daughter-in-law of R.J.G. Collins. For this, its third postal outing to date, the kiwi combined attractiveness, ornithological accuracy and stability. The New Zealand Post Archive includes a kiwi feather, as sent to printers Bradbury Wilkinson in England to provide guidance on the correct colour for this stamp.

By now the kiwi's status as a national symbol was secure, so it was the logical choice to join a koala in a cuppa around a campfire on Australia's 1988 Bicentenary stamp. Designed by a Melburnian, R. Harvey, it was issued jointly by both countries. Equally playful was 'Goldie', the official kiwi mascot which appeared on one of the stamps marking the 14th Commonwealth Games at Auckland in 1990. But the kiwi has also been required for much more formal duties, as on the official Auckland coat of arms. It was in that heraldic capacity that a pair of kiwi were depicted on R. Maurice Conly's stamp for that city's centennial in 1971.

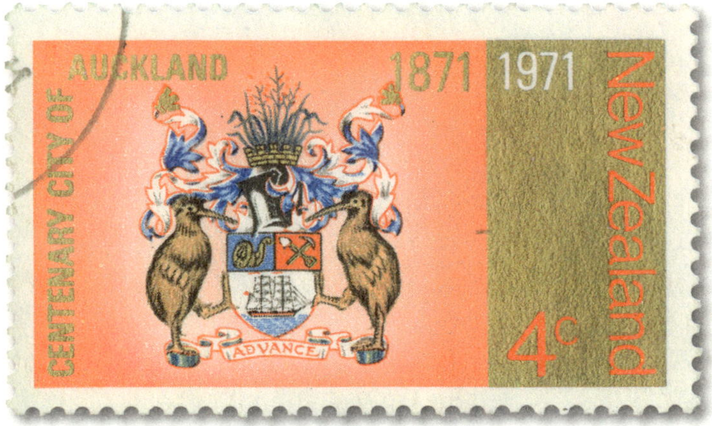

Two kiwi act as supporters on the Auckland coat of arms. This stamp, designed by R. Maurice Conly of Christchurch, marked the centenary of the City of Auckland in 1971.

Opposite: Previously depicted facing right, in 1959 the kiwi did an about-face. This bird, designed by Shirley M. Collins of Christchurch, stood for the Pan-Pacific Boy Scouts Jamboree in Auckland.

The late 1980s were especially busy for the kiwi. Just as the bird's shape had made it an ideal symbol for a well-known brand of Australian boot polish in the early 1900s, so was it the logical choice for New Zealand's first round postage stamp in 1988, designed by Allan Mitchell. In the same year the brown kiwi was one of nine bird Definitive stamps, designed by Pauline Morse of Pukerua Bay, while it later appeared in a self-adhesive version. Then in 1989 the little spotted kiwi was given top ($10) denomination in a set recognising 10 of this country's endangered birds, including the kakapo, kokako and takahe. These stamps were designed by Janet Marshall of Stratford and had been issued progressively over the previous four years.

NEW ZEALAND
HEALTH
1D.
KOTARE
2D.
POSTAGE
NEW ZEALAND
HEALTH
1D.
KOTARE
2D.
POSTAGE

Health issues during the period 1959-66 had also depicted a total of 14 different New Zealand birds but no local stamp had yet acknowledged this country's biggest bird of all, the extinct moa. It was not for lack of trying, for at least two artists had suggested it for the 1898 Pictorials. Curiously, it took another country, Cuba, to introduce the moa to postage stamps as part of a set of extinct birds ('fauna extingua') in 1974. Finally, having already attended to its endangered birds, in 1996 New Zealand issued a set of its own extinct birds, illustrating seven of the approximately 60 species which have disappeared. The giant moa, the world's tallest ever bird, was given the highest denomination ($1.80), and depicted by designer Geoffrey Cox charging headlong out of the bush. After languishing in the postal wilderness it was back, and reappeared again in 2009, when the South Island giant moa was part of a Giants of New Zealand set, designed by Dave Gunson of Auckland.

KOTARE

The mollymawk, a member of the albatross family, on the 1970 Chatham Islands issue. Designed by English-born artist Eileen Mayo.

Opposite: The 1960 Health stamps featured the kotare (kingfisher, illustrated) and the kereru (wood pigeon). Both were designed by the English printers, Bradbury Wilkinson.

24 in pursuit of science

James Cook

In 1997 New Zealand Post issued a set of stamps honouring discoverers associated with this country. Among the six voyagers were the legendary figures of Kupe, from Hawaiki, and Maui, who fished New Zealand up from the sea. Like generations of Polynesian navigators who followed, both would have drawn on their knowledge of the stars, ocean currents and flight patterns of birds to find their way across the vast Pacific.

These discovers also included Abel Tasman, who skirted this country in 1642. The next arrival was James Cook, who came ashore 157 years later. His three voyages to New Zealand had scientific objectives and during his first, on the *Endeavour*, Joseph Banks and Daniel Solander amassed large numbers of species of local plants and ferns. During the second visit, on the *Resolution* and *Adventure* in 1773, German naturalists George Forster and his son Johann studied the botany of Dusky Sound in Fiordland.

James Cook was the greatest of the Pacific explorers. He charted New

Captain Cook ashore at Poverty Bay on 8 October 1769, in the 1935 Pictorials. Original drawing for design by T.H. Jenkins.

NEW ZEALAND
CAPTAIN COOK
AT POVERTY BAY
OCTOBER 8TH 1769
2S
POSTAGE &
REVENUE

Zealand and as a result a large number of its geographical features were either named by or after him. In view of his importance it is no surprise that he has been well represented on this country's stamps. Aoraki/Mt Cook, our highest peak, was the first stamp in the 1898 Pictorial set, while Cook himself made a modest appearance in the Christchurch Exhibition set of 1906. That composition, by Louis J. Steele, bore a strong resemblance to his 1890 painting, *Arrival of Captain Cook: An incident in the Bay of Islands 29 November 1769*, a collaboration with fellow artist Kennett Watkins which is in the collection of the Auckland Art Gallery.

Cook's next postal appearance was in 1935 and on what philatelist R.J.G. Collins claimed to be 'the most interesting postage stamp of New Zealand.' It showed Cook ashore at Poverty Bay and was designed by English-born T.H. Jenkin, who came to this country in 1921.

Cook stood slightly left of centre, flanked by his officers and men, while the composition was framed on both sides by native trees and the *Endeavour*. But it was not so much the nature of the occasion, on 8 October 1769, or even the design of the stamp that attracted Collins. Alterations to the original plate, along with several printings and variations in papers, perforations and inks had combined to produce a philatelist's delight. Collins acknowledged other New Zealand stamps which appealed for similar reasons, including a 2d Full Face Queen and early Health issues—but they did not compare with the 1935 view of Cook at Poverty Bay.

Five years later Cook made his third appearance on a New Zealand stamp when a recognisable portrait was included in the 1940 Centennial set. It had been the publication of accounts of his voyages that first led to Europe's interest in this part of the Pacific. When Britain lost its American colonies it turned to Australia as a dumping ground for its convicts. As a

Captain Cook provided penny postage in the Centennial issue of 1940. James Berry's design placed the great navigator alongside the *Endeavour* and his chart of New Zealand.

result, in 1788 the First Fleet arrived in Botany Bay, so named because of the plants gathered there by Banks and Solander eight years earlier. Before long New Zealand became known for its rich resources of flax and timber, and as a popular port for whaling ships, runaway sailors and escaped convicts from across the Tasman. Lawlessness prevailed, eventually leading the British Government to declare New Zealand a Crown Colony.

The establishment of organised settlement made more systematic scientific study possible, beginning with the arrival in 1839 of geologist Dr Ernst Dieffenbach. That same year, a small fragment of bone from New Zealand caused a stir in London's scientific circles when it was delivered to leading anatomist Professor Richard Owen. He pronounced the existence of a bird, presumably extinct, that was 'nearly, if not quite, equal in size to the ostrich,' and so the world now learned about the moa. Owen was already familiar with some other peculiar features of New Zealand's natural history, including 'one of the most extraordinary and anomolous' of all birds, the kiwi.

Sir James Hector, first manager of the New Zealand Institute, which became the Royal Society of New Zealand in 1933. This stamp, designed by James Berry, was one of a pair marking the Society's centenary in 1967.

In the late 1850s two important geologists, Ferdinand von Hochstetter from Austria and Julius Haast from Germany, arrived in New Zealand. Both carried out scientific surveys around the country, while Haast became founding director of the Canterbury Museum, which opened in 1870 with an impressive display of moa skeletons. Further encouragement for local science was given by the establishment of the New Zealand Geological Survey in 1865. Its first director was Edinburgh-born James Hector, who would shortly also become manager of the recently constituted New Zealand Institute, which became known as the Royal Society of New Zealand in 1933. It marked its centenary in 1967 with two postage stamps designed by James Berry. One depicted a portrait of Sir James Hector, painted after his death (in 1945) by Christchurch artist Leonard Booth and now owned by the University of New Zealand.

The early development of science in New Zealand was heavily dependent on individuals and expertise from Europe. But the best-known and most acclaimed of all New Zealand scientists was born at Brightwater, near Nelson, in 1871. Ernest Rutherford—later Lord Rutherford—was educated at Nelson College and Canterbury University, and became known as 'the father of nuclear physics.' In 1908 he received the Nobel Prize in Chemistry, and 91 years later was included in a series of six New Zealand stamps honouring 'entrepreneurs, innovators [and] trailblazers.' Rutherford was a household name and for his next postal outing he represented the letter 'R' in the 2008 'A to Z of New Zealand' series, an alphabetical 'tiki tour' through local

1769-1969
COOK BICENTENARY
TRANSIT OF VENUS
CAPTAIN JAMES COOK
40
40
TERRA INCOGNITA
NEW ZEALAND
4c

1769-1969
COOK BICENTENARY
AE HEINO MOUWE
40
40
TOVYPOENAMMU
COOK'S CHART OF 1769
NEW ZEALAND
28c

1769-1969
COOK BICENTENARY
DR. DANIEL SOLANDER F.R.S.
RHABDOTHAMNUS SOLANDRI
MATATA
NEW ZEALAND
18c

1769-1969
COOK BICENTENARY
H.M. BARK 'ENDEAVOUR'
JOSEPH BANKS ESQ. F.R.S.
6c
NEW ZEALAND

culture and heritage. In both stamps a photograph of the famous physicist was combined with a representation of his usual subject, the inner workings of the atom.

History suggests there is one scientific event that will remain a regular theme for New Zealand stamps. In 1969 the bicentenary of Cook's first voyage was commemorated with four stamps, presenting profile portraits of the captain and his two leading scientists, Banks and Solander, along with Queen Elizabeth II. Designed by Eileen Mayo, these were an effective combination of art and science. Since then, Cook was a natural inclusion in the Discoverers set of 1997. At the very least he can anticipate further such recognition in 2019, on the 250th anniversary of his first visit to New Zealand.

Mt Aspiring, symbolising high scientific endeavour, on the 4c Royal Society of New Zealand Centennial stamp of 1967. Designed by James Berry.

Opposite: The Bicentenary of Cook's first voyage to New Zealand was marked by a set of four stamps in 1969. They also honoured the two scientists who sailed on the *Endeavour*, Sir Joseph Banks and Dr David Solander. Designed by Eileen Mayo.

25

a matter of design

pictorial approaches

New Zealand stamp design came in for some harsh criticism from artist Eric Lee-Johnson in 1951. With the exception of Britain, he considered the standard of stamps throughout the commonwealth to be 'somewhere about the lowest in the world,' while in this country it was 'painfully close to bankruptcy.' He had approved of New Zealand's first stamp design, the Full Face Queen of 1855, but found most since to be 'poor' and 'crude productions.'

Lee-Johnson identified the basic problem as a shortage of good designers. This situation encouraged 'the most wildly ambitious compositions' and 'giant-canvas subjects,' which were totally unsuitable for small postage stamps. As examples of what he termed a 'micro-photographic' approach, he identified the unfortunate 1900 South African (Boer) War (pp. 30 & 31) and 1906 Christchurch Exhibition (pp. 42–49) issues, both designed by artists who were better known for their larger scale oil paintings. But such

James Berry's interpretation of a greenstone hei tiki first appeared as the 1/6 stamp in the 1960 Pictorials. It was decimalised in 1967 and later reissued with a green background (left).

15c
TIKI
NEW ZEALAND

artists could produce good stamp designs and Lee-Johnson held up two by H. Linley Richardson as fine examples, while he also admired the 1901 Universal Penny Postage (which was designed in England) and I.F. Calder's 1935 stamp based on Maori door panel decoration.

Other problems Lee-Johnson found with New Zealand's stamps were the 'uninspired and amateurish figure composition' and 'redundant, ungainly borders and arty panels.' But things were not about to improve, for he found little merit in the most recently released stamps, the 'unimaginatively planned' and 'in places … hopelessly cluttered' Canterbury and Otago Centennial sets. His criticism was directed at the judging process as much as the designers, for he felt it too much to expect Post and Telegraph Department officials and philatelists to be sufficiently qualified to comment on aesthetic matters. The solution, he believed, was a council of New Zealanders who recognised good design and who could advise government departments on all such matters, whether it involved stamps, chairs or washing machines.

New Zealand had first recognised the promotional potential of its own postage stamps in 1895, but Lee-Johnson now warned that the country was not judged on beautiful scenery ('so laboriously depicted') alone. There were also cultural standards to be considered and these were reflected in the quality of its designing. Since then, the stamps of New Zealand have undergone dramatic changes, both in quality and quantity, the former demanding an increase in the simplicity and restraint that Lee-Johnson had found so lacking.

As alternatives to portrait heads of reigning monarchs, the 1898 Pictorials were a major break with tradition. Not surprisingly, South Island mountain scenery featured prominently at the outset. It continued with another version of Aoraki/Mt Cook, now accompanied by the North Island's Mt Taranaki/ Egmont, on the Second Pictorials in 1935. The horizontal format was ideal for such panoramic views and may have had the practical advantage of being a more convenient shape for the top of an envelope. But the vertical format was better suited for certain features of the landscape, such as Tane Mahuta in 1940 (p. 133), and the Sutherland Falls and Pohutu Geyser in 1960. Interestingly, for their first four decades, Health stamps also had a decided preference for the vertical rather than horizontal format.

New Zealand's third set of Pictorials, in 1960, demonstrated the challenge of achieving effective design on a small scale. While James Berry had conveyed the size and grandeur of a giant kauri two decades earlier, he was now much less successful with his heavily foreshortened log and its disproportionate background. Another stamp in that same set, showing butter emerging from a churn, also demonstrated the difficulty of attaining a convincing likeness. Several designs now amply demonstrated the advantages of a single subject set against a plain background, as in the depiction of the New Zealand

Two stamps from the 1960 Pictorials (decimalised 1967): 1/- timber industry, designed by James Berry; 2/6 butter making, designed by Leonard C. Mitchell.

Opposite: New Zealand's highest waterfall, the Sutherland Falls in Fiordland National Park, designed by Leonard C. Mitchell for the 5/- stamp.

A taniwha, a mythical monster, based on an early Maori rock drawing in a limestone cave in South Canterbury. Designed by D.F. Kee for the 1960 Pictorials.

flag (9d), greenstone tiki (1/6) and, in particular, the Maori rock drawing (2/-).

In general there has been a steady shift away from the cluttered and symbol-laden designs of the late 19th century. In addition to improvements made possible by printing technology, the main development has been one of simplification and the use of economical means in place of excessive or unnecessary detail. As part of this evolution, postage stamps have become less like miniature picture postcards and more like small posters. In a world awash with visual distractions, these little images need to be seen and have an instant impact. And like posters, they may exploit the eye-catching potential of strong and contrasting colours, while plain backgrounds give emphasis to the main subject. The native birds are among the subjects which have benefitted from this approach, as seen by a comparison of their earliest depictions and the more recent issues of endangered and extinct species in 1985 and 1996. They have been liberated from ornamental surroundings, and returned to their natural habitats. They are more visually accessible and (notwithstanding their real-life predicament) appear both more lively and more lifelike.

The other significant change to the postage stamps of New Zealand has been their rapid growth in numbers. On occasions prior to the early 1960s there was, at most, only one new issue per year, apart from the obligatory

The highly stylised lighthouses designed by Allan Mitchell for the Government Life Insurance Office issue of 1981.

Left: A graphic representation of Mt Taranaki/Egmont towering over Egmont National Park, in the 1970-71 Definitives, designed by Joh Enschede en Zonen, printers, Haarlem, Holland.
Right: The dynamic 1964 Road Safety stamp, in support of Accident Free Day, was designed by Leonard C. Mitchell.

Health set, but there are now regularly upwards of 18 new issues. New Zealanders wishing to post some small reflection of their country overseas are now spoilt for choice. With this proliferation, themes have diversified in the extreme, and bear little relation to such old regulars as reigning monarchs and picturesque scenery. Once dictated by postal authorities and tradition, stamp themes are now largely responsive to the market. And as a result they offer a much more informal insight into the national character and interests, dealing with such concerns as racehorses (1996), café culture (2005) and kiwi expressions (eg. 'Bit of a dag' and 'She'll be right', 2007). Such concepts would have been unthinkable back in 1895, when the call went out for stamp designs that were 'representative of New Zealand.'

sources

a. general sources & further reading:

www.stamps.nzpost.co.nz/Cultures/en-NZ/Stamps/StampsHistoricalIssues/
Tye, J.R. 'Berry, Reginald George James 1906-1979'. *Dictionary of New Zealand Biography*, updated 22 June 2007 www.dnzb.govt.nz/
—*The Image Maker: The Art of James Berry*, Hodder and Stoughton, Auckland, 1984, 46-7, 122-3
R. Maurice Conly and Paul Harrison, *Send for the Artist … Maurice Conly*, Random House, Auckland, 1995
Margaret Forde, *Another Way of Looking: New Zealand's birds on stamps*, David Bateman, Auckland, 1989
Luit Bieringa, *Postal Impressions*, New Zealand Post, Wellington, 1990
Laurie Franks, *All the Stamps of New Zealand*, A.H. & A.W. Reed, 1981
Michael Smythe, 'Post Impressions', *ProDesign*, 101, AGM Publishing, Auckland, 2009

b. sources by chapter

1.

The Times, 18 July 1837
The Southern Cross, 20 July 1855
New Zealander, 19 February 1851
Evening Post, 4 March 1882, 14 January 1891, 6 January 1897
Inangahua Times, 19 January 1891

2.

New Zealand Gazette, 21 March 1895
Evening Post, 22 March 1895, 6 August 1895, 17 August 1895, 5 September 1895, 6 September 1895, 4 January 1898, 28 January 1901, 1 July 1898, 5 July 1899, 18 November 1899

3.

R.A. Loughnan, *The Remarkable Life Story of Sir Joseph Ward: 40 years a liberal*, New Century Press, Wellington, 1929: 179
Michael Bassett, *Sir Joseph Ward: A political biography*, Auckland University Press. 1993: 111
Evening Post, 29 December 1900, 2 January 1901, 3 January 1901
Southland Times, 2 January 1901
Poverty Bay Herald, 2 January 1901
Auckland Star, 3 January 1901
The Times, 2 March 1901

4.

Alexander de Kort, *The Great Exhibition: Some Facts, Assumptions and Queries Pertaining to the Philatelic Aspects of the New Zealand International Exhibition which was held in Hagley Park, Christchurch, from the 1st of November, 1906 until the 15th of April, 1907*, Christchurch, 1985: 12
Evening Post, 16 April 1907
West Coast Times, 7 November 1906
Poverty Bay Herald, 13 November 1906

5.

New Zealand Illustrated Magazine, 1 February 1901
Evening Post, 2 February 1901, 27 September 1907, 7 May 1910, 10 May 1910
Colonist, 4 February 1901

6.

New Zealand Parliamentary Debates, June-July 1926: 979-980
Evening Post, 9 May 1910, 22 June 1911, 23 June 1911, 7 August 1915

7.

The Times, 31 July 1919, 2 December 1919, 23 December 1919,
Ashburton Guardian, 12 November 1919, 23 January 1920, 5 February 1920, 22 April 1920
Grey River Argus, 3 February 1920

8.

Otautau Standard and Wallace County Chronicle, 5 November 1929, 11 November 1932, 29 November 1932
New Zealand Truth, 17 October 1929
Tennant, Margaret. 'Gunn, Elizabeth Catherine 1879-1963'. *Dictionary of New Zealand Biography,* updated 22 June 2007 www.dnzb.govt.nz
New Zealand Parliamentary Debates, vol. 224: 614
Margaret Tennant, *Children's Health, the Nation's Wealth: A history of children's health camps*, Bridget Williams Books and Historical Branch, Dept of Internal Affairs, Wellington, 1994: 83-89, 217-223, 350-255

9.

Timaru Herald, 21 January 1889
Otago Witness, 25 January 1889
Thames Star, 17 July 1899
Evening Post, 20 July 1899, 19 September 1899
www.teara.govt.nz/en/nearshore-islands/3/5
www.blennerhassettfamilytree.com/New-Zealand-Airmail-Postage-Stamps/
www.airmailsnz.com/
www.nzstamps.org.uk/air/regular/westland.html

10.

West Coast Times, 3 August 1867
Otago Witness, 29 March 1900
Evening Post, 13 December 1895
A. Dibley, *New Zealand Arms Type Duty Stamps: The design process, 1915-1929*, Royal Philatelic Society of New Zealand, Wellington, 1988

11.

R.A. Falla, 'The Tuatara', *Bulletin of The Auckland Zoological Society* (Inc), No.2, October 1935: 3-5
Frieda Cobb Blanchard, 'Tuatara: "Living Fossils" Walk on Well-Nigh Inaccessible Rocky Islands off the Coast of New Zealand', *National Geographic Magazine*, May 1935: 649-662

12.

New Zealand Herald, 17 April 1935, 1 May 1935

13.

Ashburton Guardian, 27 April 1915
Poverty Bay Herald, 30 April 1915, 22 January 1919
Evening Post, 29 April 1915, 4 May 1915

14.

New Zealand Parliamentary Debates, 12 December 1936
New Zealand Herald, 11 May 1937, 12 May 1937, 13 May 1937, 14 May 1937

15.

New Zealand Centennial News, Department of Internal Affairs, Wellington, Nos. 7 (30 March 1939) – 13 (1 April 1940)
New Zealand Herald, 2 January 1940, 4 January 1940
William Renwick (editor), *Creating a National Spirit: Celebrating New Zealand's Centennial*, Victoria University Press, 2004: 56

16.
The Times, 7 June 1946
Auckland Star, 1 April 1946
17.
J.W. Brodie, *A History of Government Life Postage Stamps, New Zealand Government Life Insurance Corporation and Royal Philatelic Society of New Zealand,* Wellington, 1988
C.W. Vennell, *Tower of Strength: A centennial history of the New Zealand Government Life Insurance Office, 1869-1969,* 1969
Wellington Independent, 26 February 1870
Otago Witness, 30 April 1891
Wanganui Herald, 8 September 1891
18.
The Press, 23 November 1950, 27 November 1950, 28 November 1950, 8 December 1950, 20 December 1950
J.R. Tye, *The Image Maker: The art of James Berry,* Hodder and Stoughton, Auckland, 1984: 50
19.
New Zealand Herald, 1 October 1943
Auckland Star, 1 October 1943, 5 October 1943, 1 November 1951, 2 November 1951
20.
J.R. Tye, *The Image Maker: The art of James Berry,* Hodder and Stoughton, Auckland, 1984: 46-7, 122-3
21.
D. Robertson (compiler), *Early History of the New Zealand Post Office,* Wellington, 1905: 11
Howard Robinson, *A History of the Post Office in New Zealand,* Government Printer, Wellington, 1964: 69
New Zealand Herald, 19 June 1953
22.
New Zealand Herald, 15 February 1957
Brookes, Barbara. 'King, Frederic Truby 1858-1938'. *Dictionary of New Zealand Biography,* updated 22 June 2007 www.dnzb.govt.nz/
www.guardian.co.uk/artanddesign/2009/jun/16/obituary-michael-goaman/
23.
southseas.nla.gov.au/journals/banks/17700117.html
Margaret Forde, *Another Way of Looking: New Zealand's birds on stamps*, David Bateman, Auckland, 1989: 13
24.
A.H. McLintock (editor), *An Encyclopaedia of New Zealand,* Government Printer, Wellington, 1966, vol. 3: 179-181
http://collections.tepapa.govt.nz/exhibitions/jameshector/segment.aspx?irn=105
R.J.G. Collins, *The 2s Pictorial of 1935-1942: A detailed study of plate 1,* Verne, Collins & Co., Ltd., Christchurch, 1951: 3-7
25.
Eric Lee-Johnson, 'New Zealand Postage Stamp Design', *Year Book of the Arts in New Zealand*, 1951, Harry H. Tombs Ltd., Wellington, No. 7: 91-96
Michael Smythe, 'Post Impressions', *ProDesign, 101*, AGM Publishing, Auckland, 2009

Illustration credits

The following items are from: Museum of New Zealand Te Papa Tongarewa; The New Zealand Post Museum Collection, Gift of New Zealand Post Ltd, 1992

page 10. Original line drawing for 6d Express; Delivery stamp, 1939; James Berry; Wellington; 228 x 291 mm; Registration number: TMP011034

page 20. Original watercolour design; (unaccepted) for 2½d Queen Victoria; Second Sideface stamp, 1891; A. E. Cousins, Wellington; 45 x 36 mm Registration number: TMP011052

page 22. Original watercolour design; (accepted) for 2½d Queen Victoria; Second Sideface stamp, 1891; A. E. Cousins, Wellington; 45 x 37 mm Registration number: TMP011074

page 23. Original watercolour design (unaccepted) for 2½d Queen Victoria; Second Sideface stamp, 1891; A. E. Cousins, Wellington; 45 x 36 mm Registration number: TMP011053

page 30. Original artwork (ink) for 1½d Empire's Call stamp, 1900; James M. Nairn, New Zealand; 180 x 277 mm; Registration number: PH000074

page 46. Original watercolour artwork for Christchurch Exhibition stamps, 1906; Louis J. Steele, Auckland; 69 x 67 mm (left), 69 x 67 mm (centre) and 68 x 68 mm (right); Registration number: TMP011036

page 58. Original line drawing for 2/- George V Admiral Definitive stamp, 1926; H. Linley Richardson, Wellington 266 x 237 mm; Registration number: TMP011051

page 65. Original wash drawings for 1d Victory stamp, 1920; Thomas De La Rue & Company, London; 30 x 24 mm Registration number: TMP011050

page 68. Original wash drawing for 3d Victory stamp, 1920; Thomas De La Rue & Company, London; 24 x 36 mm Registration number: TMP011046

page 70. Original wash drawing for 1½d Victory stamp, 1920; Thomas De La Rue & Company, London; 24 x 31 mm; Registration number: TMP011046

page 76. Original wash drawing for 1d Hygeia Health stamp, 1932; William J. Cooch, Wellington; 280 x 194 mm Registration number: TMP011039

page 76. Original line drawing for 1d Hygeia Health stamp, 1932; William J. Cooch, Wellington; 283 x 184 mm Registration number: TMP011040

page 96. Original wash drawing for 8d Tuatara Pictorial stamp, 1935; Leonard C. Mitchell, Wellington; 256 x 226 mm Registration number: TMP011037

page 86. Rough pencil design for 6d Airmail stamp, 1935; James Berry, Wellington; 180 x 273 mm; Registration number: TMP011038

page 96. Original line drawing for 8d Tuatara Pictorial stamp, 1935; Leonard C. Mitchell, Wellington; 182 x 158 mm; Registration number: TMP011042

page 98. Original line drawing for 1/- Tui Pictorial stamp, 1935; Leonard C. Mitchell, Wellington; 143 x 119 mm; Registration number: TMP011044

page 110. Original colour artwork for 9d Maori panel Pictorial stamp, 1935; I. Calder, Wellington; 106 x 127 mm; Registration number: TMP011043

page 110. Original line drawing for 9d Maori panel Pictorial stamp, 1935; I. Calder, Wellington; 204 x 160 mm; Registration number: TMP011041

page 116. Original line drawing for 1d ANZAC stamp, 1936; Leonard C. Mitchell, Wellington; 205 x 121 mm; Registration number: TMP011048

page 116. Photograph of soldier used for design of ANZAC stamps, 1936; Photographer unknown; Reproduction from an original print mounted on an album page; Registration number: TMP011047

page 128. Original border design (unaccepted) for George VI Definitive stamps, 1938; Unknown designer; 128 x 72 mm; Registration number: TMP011030

page 134. Original line drawing for 4d Centennial stamp, 1940; Leonard C. Mitchell, Wellington; 150 x 247 mm Registration number: TMP011035

page 146. Original pencil drawing for 4d Government Life Insurance stamp, 1947; James Berry, Wellington; 263 x 195 mm; Registration number: TMP011032

page 151. Original pencil drawing for 3d Government Life Insurance stamp, 1947 James Berry, Wellington; 262 x 197 mm; Registration number: TMP011033

page 152. Original pencil drawing for ½d Government Life Insurance stamp, 1947; James Berry, Wellington; 213 x 263 mm; Registration number: TMP011031

page 185. Original wash drawing for 2d Postage Stamp Centenary stamp, 1955; R. Maurice Conly, Wellington; 173 x 149 mm; Registration number: TMP011049

index